THE LAW

OF

HISTORY

THE LAW OF HISTORY

Volume I

THE UNIVERSAL LOGIC OF THE HUMAN MIND

Christophe Scheidhauer

Frontispiece: *The Discovery of History* ©

The Law of History © 2021 Christophe Scheidhauer, Paris

Acknowledgments: Figure 4 : Gallica/ BNF ; Figure 5 : Institut Pasteur - Musée Pasteur ; Figure 6 & 7 : Wikimedia Commons, Figure 14: Anhrefn/Canolfan Sain ; Figure 15 : Musée Jacquemart-André ; Figure 19: Walker Art Gallery, Liverpool ; Figure 20 : Musée National de Malmaison ; Figure 21 : Alte Pinakothek ; Figure 22 : The J. Paul Getty Museum.

First edition March 2022 - Foundation Books

5.5*8.5 in ; paperback

Kindle Direct Publishing, Seattle, Washington

ISBN : 979-8-4144-7407-4

Library of Congress Control Number: 2022903044

To Guillaume

Contents

The Revolution of Human Science

Three-hundred years ago a visionary researcher launched a scientific revolution. His name was John Locke. He set out to explain our world on a completely new basis. This was 1690, the dawn of the Age of Enlightenment. People generally thought that their world was managed by unpredictable supernatural forces. Locke supposed on the contrary that the destiny of humanity fundamentally depended on the earthly logic of our human minds.

He believed that our world had been created once and for all, and was therefore governed by universal and permanent laws. He conceived of the human mind accordingly. Locke designed simple and coherent hypotheses to explain how our ideas constantly develop and organize themselves. He concluded that the human mind is itself an autonomous universe which possesses its own logic. This discovery he published in *An Essay Concerning Human Understanding*.

In 1687, as Locke was writing the manuscript of his book, his vision received powerful confirmation by one of his own countrymen, Isaac Newton. The physicist revealed the *Principles* that explain the movements of all objects, on Earth as in the skies. He subjected the heavens to the same laws as our human lives on Earth. There could be no more supernatural beings out there to rule our lives, the gods that people and astrology had for millennia sought to observe in celestial movements. Everything has to obey a single determination.

Locke and Newton had invented a new vision of the world, a world that could be explored by observation and conceived by the power of the human mind. This initial triumph inspired and emboldened generations of researchers, in "natural" as in "human" sciences.

Locke's general theory of the human mind became the foundation on which David Hume, as early as 1739, endeavored to lay the foundations of a "compleat system of the sciences."[1] He started with proposing to reveal the logic of scientific discoveries. He continued with an attempt at explaining everything in our human world, from the most fleeting and intimate notions to the most permanent institutions.

This vision is, in retrospect, all the more fascinating considering that Locke and Hume were pioneers. As such, they could only access very limited observations, especially compared to the ones that are presently available to us. Records, when they existed at all, rarely allowed complex comparisons or trend analysis. There was actually no account of any historical fact beyond the ancient Greeks. Early civilizations were completely unknown, like prehistory. Even for more recent periods, there was no method for distinguishing between legend and fact, myth and history. Archeology did not exist. The deciphering of ancient writings was still to come. Knowledge of countries beyond Europe was extremely limited. Scientists knew very little of the relations between languages; linguistics and philology had barely emerged at all. Detailed description of brain tissues and activities would not be available before the late nineteenth century. Neuroscience was still far in the future. Locke and Hume, like their immediate followers, could only work from their own direct observations and the relatively rare books which were available to them. In that context, their ambitions and, even more, their results, are truly admirable.

Inspired by such a start, their successors relentlessly explored our human world, our history and our minds and revealed, over the next three hundred years, societies, times and dimensions that neither Locke nor Hume had ever contemplated.

In the seventeenth century, the nations that populated the world seemed at the time to have been there since the world's creation. Nowadays, any primary school student learns about a time when none of these nations even existed. They take for granted a much deeper past. They are familiar with ancient civilizations, and also with prehistory, and with the existence of extinct human species. They even know of ages when not a single human roamed this world, and are aware of times that preceded life itself.

None of this would have been thinkable in the seventeenth century. But particularly unimaginable to a person of that time, twenty-first century students learn, without even thinking about it, how recent and evolving our own knowledge is. They are immersed in the description of a dynamic, changing world. This conception was completely inaccessible to seventeenth- and early eighteenth-century scientists. It was, however, ushered in by the scientific revolution that they designed. We are their heirs. They allowed us to inherit three hundred years of tremendous scientific progress.

And yet we have forgotten how much we owe them. We have forgotten their project to build a complete, coherent understanding of the human mind and of the human world. We have almost unanimously renounced the possibility of developing a predictive, scientific approach in this field. It is as if the more our knowledge of human history had progressed, and the more the new generations had abandoned the ideal of their predecessors.

As a result, in spite of its incredible successes, human science has gradually been deconsidered until, in the twenty-first century, "science" became a synonym for "natural" sciences. "Humanities" have been almost completely reduced to specialties belonging to the arts or to politics. By all accounts, the human mind itself is too unpredictable to be a truly scientific object.

But that opinion is not well-founded. The human mind is a scientific object. It can be explained by observation and logic. There was no reason to renounce. In fact, human sciences have gone through a very long crisis that is about to end, because it had everything to do with the deep logic of major scientific discoveries.

The logic of scientific discoveries

The logic of scientific discoveries was only exposed for the first time in 1962, by Thomas Kuhn. He observed that scientific research is not always such as it presents itself to the public: a linear progress of knowledge. The accumulation of observations does not always result in the emergence of ever more powerful theories. Science actually goes through long cycles. Some periods present the appearances of an orderly progress. But they alternate with tremendous crises that lead to "scientific revolutions" and periods of renewed progress. During "scientific revolutions", received theories are completely revised and replaced by completely new ones.

Kuhn discovered that these upheavals were due to the very structure of scientific knowledge. Indeed, theories and hypotheses shared in a research field are all based on a "general theory" from which all others depend. This general theory provides a whole research community with a common vision of the world and determines what is scientifically correct in the field. Kuhn named the general theory a "paradigm,"[2] a name which became an instant hit. It is now consensually accepted that a scientific "revolution"[3] means a "paradigm change" or first-order change: a new paradigm is proposed and the ancient paradigm is abandoned. All theories are reexamined. Individual theories survive the scientific revolution depending on whether they fit the new paradigm, the new general theory.

Kuhn's book, *The Structure of Scientific Revolutions*, was itself a revolution in the conception of science. It was the first book to explain science realistically, as a dynamic process, a continuous research made by a community of people rather than as an abstract, fixed state of knowledge. For this reason, Kuhn's work faced many critics. They particularly disliked being told that ancient theories, which they scorned and classified as unscientific, had initially obeyed the same methods as the theories that came to survive scientific revolutions.[4] In their eyes, that aspect of Kuhn's observations discredited the whole scientific process. Their objections are probably the reason Kuhn elected the more neutral "paradigm" to name ancient and obsolete general theories. The critics were absurd, of course. Science is not static, but a permanent research, a permanent "quest."[5]

The scientific quest answers a deeply shared logic. All scientists desire to discover the ultimate principle, the one "law," "algorithm" or "formula" that explains everything in our world. This is why they are fascinated by a general theory which seem to uphold such a principle.

Paradoxically, this fundamental quest is rarely explicit in real scientific exchanges. Each wants to make the discovery themselves; they would not encourage anyone else in that direction. It is at best alluded to, as when a senior colleague regrets they did not yet have time to complete their "big book." By contrast, it can be very explicit in fiction, because authors of fiction do not compete in the scientific arena. Goethe's character Faust, emphatically regretted that he had not discovered the "core principle that holds the world together."[6] In *The Theory of Everything,* the young Steven Hawking bashfully explained to his fiancée that we scientists seek the "one single unifying equation that explains everything in the universe."[7] The first quote from *Faust* dates from 1808, while Hawking's is from 2014. It is an enduring cause indeed.

The pursuit of the ultimate unifying principle governs all scientific activities. All general theories are based on a general principle that seems to fulfill the quest at the time the theory is proposed. For example, Copernicus's revolution was based on the principle that the Sun was the real center of all planetary movement. Newton's revolution was based on the principle of universal gravitation. Darwin's revolution was based on the natural selection of the fittest. Einstein's general relativity was based on the principle that light is always observed to travel at the same speed.

The pursuit of the ultimate unifying principle also suffices to explain scientific crises and revolutions. The discovery of "anomalies" or "problems,"[8] observations that the general principle cannot explain, can decisively discredit a paradigm and prepare the way for a new one. The discovery of anomalies detaches a rising number of scientists from previous conceptions and the advent of a new principle eventually unifies a new field, just like Kuhn observed.

The new unifying principle not only covers the facts explained by the ancient one, but makes also sense of the previous anomalies.[9] This was for example why Copernicus's explanation of the movements of the planets and the stars replaced Ptolemy's from the sixteenth century on. Copernicus's model allowed for many new observations that Ptolemy's could not. Ptolemy's model was actually very complex. It necessitated a specific explanation for the motion of each planet. And so any new observation would likely jeopardize the whole. Copernicus's was much simpler than Ptolemy's. It could easily accommodate new observations. Anomalies were much less likely. Much simpler, it eventually opened the way for a unified theory of motion in our universe.

Science is thus about discovering and defending a simpler, more coherent explanation that covers a greater range of observations. Scientific revolutions are how more powerful and efficient general theories can emerge; they are necessary to the exploration of our world and to the decipherment of the causes that govern all events.

Kuhn published his masterpiece in the 1960s. He was mostly inspired by physics, biology, chemistry and astronomy, the most prestigious scientific fields at the time. Since Newton, natural sciences had gone from triumph to triumph. Physics, chemistry and biology had repeatedly discovered elegant solutions to the most daunting problems. Each of these disciplines had converged upon a powerful unifying theory. Meanwhile, human sciences had accumulated observations and uncovered an increasingly complex world and history, but at the same time, they did not appear anymore capable of producing a coherent explanation of the world they uncovered. The research fields seem to diverge ever farther.

Since the 1960s, scientific research has continued to progress. Its developments have since confirmed the phases in scientific production that Kuhn had uncovered. Physics has moved on and entered a new cycle. Gone are the days when the dream of unifying all the forces of physics was deemed to be within reach. It has withered away with the discovery of major anomalies in "dark matter" and "dark energy." They signaled the beginning of a new phase of crisis.

Biology followed an almost parallel curve. Darwinian biology had just triumphed in the 1960s following the discovery of the molecular structure of DNA in the 1950s, the molecule that explained heredity and the emergence, through genetic mutations, of new qualities generation after generation. In the 2020s, it is generally accepted that viruses carry genetic material along with DNA and RNA. Genetic inheritance has been observed to often occur independently from reproduction, through viral transmission. Darwin's elegant Tree of Life has seemingly transformed into an inextricable bush.[10]

Scientific research follows creative cycles where theory unifications alternate with crises, one phase providing the fuel for the next one. No field is exempt from these dynamics. The prolonged crisis entered by human science may not be fatal after all. As for other scientific fields, whether it can produce a coherent, fact-based, predictive explanation of our world depends on whether we can understand and solve the fundamental problem it faces.

The Fundamental Problem

Locke's general theory of the human mind seemed infallible. It encouraged generations of scientists to bravely venture into unchartered domains. It is based on just one hypothesis: a mind organizing itself spontaneously and autonomously by associations of ideas nourished from its own experiences. The principle is still the consensually accepted foundation of contemporary human science, a principle confirmed by countless observations and experiments.

However, Locke added a second hypothesis. He derived it from the first and presented it as equivalent. The second hypothesis states that there can be no "innate ideas," ideas that any human would inevitably nurture.[11] This means, in particular, no universal ideas. It makes sense, it seems: each mind develops from its own experience. No two life experiences are entirely similar, no not people can come up with exactly the same ideas. Therefore, there can be no ideas that are universally innate. The argument seems irrefutable. But observations tell us something different.

Anomalies were detected early. Hume himself (1739) had to contend with multiple cases of universal ideas.[12] These anomalies were originally not deemed important though. They must have seemed a secondary problem that would resolve itself with time and could not threaten the rigorous logic of Locke's hypotheses. After all, even a thinker as eminent as Kant (1781) had tried to argue that some notions, like space, should be universal because they would be necessary to think. But he did not present a clear and convincing alternative to Locke's hypotheses.[13]

However, the problem of universally innate ideas became much more vexatious as human science developed in directions wholly unforeseen in the seventeenth century, especially as it revealed a much more complex history of humanity.

The researchers who dealt with language, law or history, frequently observed surprising similarities between events that took place in communities that claimed separate origins and different histories. This mysteriously suggested common predispositions, which Locke's second hypothesis had so emphatically ruled out.

A chasm opened between the explanation of each individual "micro"-level thoughts and action, which seemed to obey Locke's laws, and that of the "macro," large-scale, collective results of these thoughts and actions, that contradicted Locke's law. Locke's paradigm thus not only inspired a scientific community but also divided it. And the "gap" has never been bridged since.[14]

Micro-economics, for instance, developed from the late eighteenth century and considered that "economic agents" behaved according to their own individual preferences. Such a conception was fully compatible with Locke's hypotheses. Most micro-level theories, in economics and elsewhere, duly emphasized "rigor," which meant loyalty to the paradigm. Meanwhile, macro-level theories mostly appealed to realism instead. Some research fields, like macro-linguistics, started developing their own laws, which bore no relations with Locke's hypotheses.

This early division was soon exacerbated as scientists acquired an ever deeper knowledge of the past. A whole new vision of human history emerged, one of a dynamic world, where everything permanently transforms, even the elements that had hitherto been deemed the most stable: nations, states and languages. Change started to be regarded as permanent. This dynamic world called ever more for an explanation which could only be found in a universal principle, a universal structure of the human mind.

However, no such unifying principle was revealed. Independent hypotheses and research fields therefore emerged as discoveries multiplied. Deepening fragmentation only seemed to further compromise the formulation of a unifying theory. Tentative re-unifications only created new sub-fields of research.

The fragmentation of human science has become its most defining feature. By contrast, all physicists or all biologists share a "paradigm" and a fundamental research program. Not all physicists have read books that came to embody these paradigms, the *Principles* of Newton (1687)[15] and the *Relativity* of Einstein (1920).[16] Neither have all biologists have read their own paradigm, the *Origins* of Darwin (1859).[17] But in these fields all students are taught the principles originally proposed by those authors. In consequence, discoveries made by any physicist or any biologist can be related to the research conducted by any colleague. Associated journals, conferences and associations offer ventures where such discoveries can be shared and valorized. This is not the case anymore in human sciences. They presently exist only in the plural. There are no more principles and theories unifying them.

There are frequent calls to encourage interdisciplinary research though. But researchers are increasingly "specialized", confined by academic discipline to an ever narrower field, and those who can bridge different fields have become extremely rare. The project of a unified theory is being abandoned. Nothing sums up better the present mood than the confessions of a leading economist who candidly admitted he would have preferred to be a "psychohistorian,"[18] a scientist using a working general theory to predict the future and save humanity. But to him it was only a childish desire, forever confined to Asimov's science-fiction series.

A unifying paradigm seems to be a project consigned, for all practical purposes, to the realm of the philosophy of science: something that should ideally exist but that cannot be translated in actual research programs.[19] Pursuing an academic career in human science nowadays seems to imply an acceptation that the unified theory must forever remain a dream. In that context, few would probably support the opinion that "humanities" are on the verge of a revolution and would become once more a powerful and predictive science.

Yet applying Kuhn's model to human science indicates that we should not discard so rapidly three hundred years of exploration, observation, collection and classification. After all, previous scientific discoveries also depended upon a long accumulation of facts that initially appeared to produce many more problems than solutions. A millennium of astronomical records was necessary to initiate the Copernican revolution and replace Ptolemy's vision of the universe. Without the cumulated works of Copernicus, Kepler and Galileo, Newton's laws would have been neither imaginable nor testable. A century of collection and classification of rocks and soils, fossils and species prepared the Darwinian synthesis. And Einstein's re-foundation of physics also finds its material in the accumulation of observations made during the previous decades.

In spite of the appearances, Locke's problem could actually possess a solution. Minds that self-organize and that structure themselves after their own specific experiences could produce universal ideas, even if it is apparently counter-intuitive. And we might be much more advanced than most think on the way towards a solution. Providing we can bridge the many fields of research that have become inaccessible to one another.

Towards the Solution

The mind seems to be the most complex object in the universe, an unfathomable number of simultaneous events, countless ideas in permanent reprocessing. To reduce it to a single structure seems beyond our power. Many scientists continue to disseminate that paralyzing vision. We have to get beyond it. There are ways to analyze the structure of the mind.

Gravitation can never be observed directly either. It is observed through its effects on objects, through their relative motions. It was induced from observations as the only possible explanation. Likewise, natural selection can only be observed through the record of fossil and living species. If there is a structure of the mind, it must leave a distinct trace on the way people talk, write, act and produce. There should be a universal way people express their ideas and act upon them. Based on that reasoning, our predecessors actually almost solved the problem. They came very close, no less than three times.

First, a network of researchers, among them Rank,[20] Barthes[21] and Lévi-Strauss[22] observed that all stories have something in common. They identified a universal structure in tales, legends and myths. Rank demonstrated as early as 1905 that this universal structure meant that there was a universal structure of the human mind.[23]

A second network of researchers, spearheaded by Kondratiev[24] and Goldstein,[25] analyzed economic and political cycles and observed that all human activities tended to synchronize. There is a universal dynamics in human activities. Kondratiev deduced as early as 1926 from this observation that a law could be proposed that would explain all events.[26]

Last but not least, Noam Chomsky observed that all humans share an ability to develop new languages, new ways of effectively communicating with one another. He concluded in 1969 that it demonstrated that the human mind possesses a "universal" capacity to generate language.[27]

Even if each mind develops from its own unique experiences, it universally develops in a similar way and entertains as a result universal ideas. Before Rank, Kondratiev and Chomsky, this seemed impossible. Thanks to them, we know that Locke's problem must possess a solution.

The problem remained unsolved to this day though. The many breakthroughs of our predecessors did not lead to a definitive identification of the universal structure of the human mind.

Observations and explanations were incomplete. The different groups of researchers were mutually unaware of their discoveries. They never connected them. The fragmentation of human science had taken its toll. It was entrenched in hypotheses which limited the possibilities and set boundaries between fields.

For instance, the discovery of a universal structure in narrative had been the result of creative interactions between semiologists, linguists and psychologists. But in the end, like Aristotle long before them, they all considered that only fiction could express a universal structure, and that historical accounts could not. These specialists never connected with other fields, with historians or sociologists for example, to test their assumptions. Their discovery remained therefore incomplete.

Likewise, the discovery of a universal dynamics in human activities was the distinct result of a small network of economists. In that field too, the scientists who made the breakthroughs tended to explain them exclusively with the hypotheses that were available in their domain. They viewed economic life exclusively as the product of rational minds seeking to maximize their material well-being. They could not explain economics together with international conflicts, which were, on the contrary, considered to be the result of irrational, destructive impulses. And they never sought to connect with polemologists to identify a foundation on which to explain together both dimensions of the phenomenon. They rather stuck with insufficient hypotheses that were conforming to the economic worldview. The way towards the solution was barred on all sides by such limiting hypotheses. On all sides, it turned out, except one. One phenomenon would allow to identify a cause and explain all the observations of our predecessors.

All conflicts and alliances are bipolar. It seems self-evident. Everyone imagines a conflict to have two sides. No one sees a problem with that, much less a problem worthy of high-level attention. Problems must appear puzzling. They must somehow run against expectations. Bipolarization does not. People happen to behave exactly like they are expected to behave. Bipolarization was therefore never a prominent subject in human science.

Yet bipolarization is a universal dynamics in human activities. The universality and permanence of the tendency to bipolarize implies that it is driven by one and only one universal set of ideas that constantly operate on all people. Only one universal structure of the mind is possible. And its exact properties can be deduced from that of bipolarization and that of a self-organizing, autonomous mind.

This is the solution: the universal structure of the mind that explains bipolarization also explains the discoveries of our predecessors. It explains a common structure in all narratives, fictional and historical, and a general dynamics in human activities, one that drives economics like conflicts. A hidden and all-powerful logic of the human mind is the law of history.

The human mind operates as Locke described it three hundred years ago. It self-organizes from its own experiences. But it produces a fundamental set of universal ideas. This can only mean that the information conveyed by life experiences is always partly the same, regardless of the specifics. Observing human activities allows to identify which information is always carried by any event and to explain how it structures the whole mind. The mind obeys a simple, single, universal logic.

This book explains in detail each of these points. So far, not a single observation has falsified our hypothesis. For the first time, we possess a simple, working, coherent, unified theory. Our human world can be explained and described as it is. The dream of many generations has become reality. Our predecessors have been vindicated.

When I conducted my first research, I was assigned a case that no available theory could explain. Fortunately, I was constantly encouraged to keep an open mind and to cling to the facts. I took time to observe reality. I ruled out no possibility and put all available theories to the test. I tried to be true to this mindset in the following pages. I encourage you to do the same.

You will notice I personally studied some of the events that are presented in this book. This made a considerable difference. It allowed me to observe interpersonal relations in detail and to meet firsthand key witnesses. Most of them were extremely cooperative and willing to spend time evoking decisive events and personal motivations. It was a rare privilege and a precious opportunity.

I was helped by many companions along the way: first and foremost, Jean Leca, who supervised my doctoral research, and also colleagues, my parents and my wife, Karine, themselves great researchers who supported me along the way. No such endeavor can be a solitary one. Even if I alone sign this book today, I know that I carry on with the work of many generations.

I started this research more than twenty years ago, at the turn of the millennium. All these years, new disruptions have appeared in our world, and none have disappeared: the simultaneous rise of global terrorism, of financial and economic instability, of social tensions, of an international arm races. They are as many symptoms of an accelerating crisis. Violent regimes all over the globe deny truth and freedom to ever more people.

Moreover, during the same period, the human population has grown at a rhythm without precedent. We have to cooperate and manage increasingly limited resources in a sustainable way. So far, we know we have certainly fallen short.

Our time calls for renewed hope, for a reconnection with the original vision of the scientific revolution, which inspired so many to believe that progress was possible and that freedom and science would bring a better, happier future. Whether their vision becomes reality is now up to a new generation of researchers. You could be one of them.

This book is therefore written to be accessible to a general audience, so that they could in turn deliver a new golden age of innovation, not only in fundamental research, but in applied research as well.

Science is often imagined shrouded in mystery. Complexity and technology make it appear the arcane domain of a limited number of experts. But when it comes to human science, facts all too often simply hide in plain sight. All we need to explore the human world is to be wired to other people, and we all are.

The Unified Theory

We humans live in a world where everything permanently changes. Only one thing never changes, the force that sets everything in motion, our lives and our world. This force is unique and universal. It connects everything.

It is the deepest logic of the human mind, a single algorithm that ultimately commands all our thoughts and actions, and our entire mind's workings. Its existence defies intuition. Yet its manifestations are everywhere to be observed.

The Law of History reveals how the universal logic of the human mind drives all events, from the most intimate and fleeting thoughts, to the millennial rise and fall of civilizations.

Part I – The Logic of the Mind

The human mind follows a universal logic. Although life experiences may be almost infinitely diverse, the mind always treats information in a specific way. The mind thus structures itself according to a universal pattern.

The logic of the mind is binary; it must interpret events as good against evil. It must also detect wills behind all events. It therefore interprets them in the light of a heroic scenario. Each one thinks and acts as if they were the Hero of History, destined to reveal, fight and destroy the source of all evils, the Enemy.

It is the fundamental logic, the one which organizes all ideas. Yet, people cannot be conscious of it. They feel that the world is just that way; they cannot recognize that it is their mind at work. Although all their thoughts and actions betray it, they do not know that they desire above all to be the Hero of History.

This universal logic can be observed as it shapes all associations of ideas *(Part I)*, all narratives (*Part II*). It also induces a universal dynamic in human interaction and in all activities (*Parts III-V*).

Part II – To be the Hero of History

The universal logic shapes the vision of the world each one develops. From childhood to adulthood, people pursue the same fundamental goal: to save their loved ones from evil. Only the complexity of the scenario they imagine changes.

Each story, fictional or historical, is based on the same primary notions: a unique world, a unique history, and oneself, the Hero, fighting a unique, intimate, hidden Enemy.

Fiction and historical accounts differ only on one point. There is no hero in historical accounts. No one would ever pass on accounts which make someone else the Hero of History. This role, each one unknowingly reserves for themselves.

Part III – Making History

People need friends, people with whom they can share everything. Only with friends can they to feel confident, can they know right from wrong, and be certain not to be manipulated by the Enemy, who hides and manipulates his victims.

As they find companions, humans also make adversaries. Humans are social and political animals. They must build alliances, which are always bipolar. One side builds up in reaction to the other. The more they interact, the more they react to each other's moves, and discover who the Enemy really is. Unknowingly, they converge on a new vision of History and disagree only about which side is the rightful one.

The more both sides interact, the more each one can recognize good and evil, and the more easily both sides attract followers. The belief that people should be reasonable only adds to reciprocal hostility. Alliances and conflicts grow until they end up in the victory of one side and the defeat of the other. But peace never lasts. A new cycle of bipolar conflict starts as the previous one ends.

Part IV – A General Mobilization

Each one believes they are extraordinary, different from ordinary people, who would be egoistic, materialistic and greedy, and would therefore be easily bought and manipulated by the Enemy. Each one believes that they, and their companions, are the only ones to be different, because they are aware of the danger.

Each one secretly dreams of being detached from material bounds. But one must also detach ordinary people from the Enemy. To attract them to the cause one feels one must provide more goods and service than the other side. Any policy necessarily entails the production and redistribution of assets. Each one therefore believes they must achieve the highest possible material position.

As conflict intensifies, each camp seeks to enlist more supporters by outcompeting the other side in production and redistribution. Economic activities rise and fall with the conflict. All activities tend to synchronize with the bipolar confrontation.

Part V – A General Competition

Companions are allies but also rivals in a general competition for distinction. No relationship is devoid of ambiguity. It is not only about being distinguished from ordinary people. It is also a competition to be distinguished from the companions and be recognized as a superior being.

Allies must exchange special favors, services, gifts, goods and positions, and, at the same time, outcompete each other to woo new allies. Trade and investments thus follow the shifting patterns of alliances and rivalries. Prices and volume produced change with them. The whole world of business, with its specific beliefs and habits, follows cycles that contribute to the general bipolarization. Allies are eventually driven to turn against each other, despite their desire to the contrary. Eventually, tensions between companions must trigger a new conflict.

*

The universal logic of the human mind shapes all human thoughts, narratives and actions. It determines relations, both interpersonal and within large groups, and explains politics and conflicts like production and trade, in every human society.

Thus to really understand it all, one must first discover what causes the human mind to acquire this universal logic and solve, once and for all, the fundamental problem that scientists faced for centuries.

*   *   *

The book is designed to make as much use of imagination as of logic. With a simple backbone of deductive reasoning, it is mostly devoted to cases and examples. It offers a journey to the discovery of our human world, a world familiar and yet never fully observed and understood before, a world governed by a force that is hidden and yet present in everything we thing and do. The many cases make concrete the point that the theory is conclusively tested and stands unfalsified. The book also makes simple previous and alternate theories. Because an idea is always more readily understood and remembered if can be distinguished from other explanations.

The book is thus made up of three types of texts that can be recognized by their distinct styles.

The explanation itself: the law, its causes and consequences.

Short cases and examples that illustrate the explanation.

Previous theories and problems, discussed in relation with the law.

I

THE LOGIC OF THE MIND

The human mind obeys only one logic, and it is a universal one. Although life experiences may be almost infinitely diverse, the mind always treats the events in a specific way. Information thus structures itself according to a universal pattern.

The logic of the mind is binary; it must interpret events as good against evil. It must also detect wills behind all events. It therefore interprets them in the light of a heroic scenario. Each one thinks and acts as if they were the Hero of History, destined to reveal, fight and destroy the source of all evils, the Enemy.

It is the fundamental logic, the one which organizes all ideas. Yet, people cannot be conscious of it. They feel that the world is just that way; they cannot recognize that it is their mind at work. Likewise, they cannot recognize that they desire above all to be the Hero of History, even if all their thoughts and actions betray it.

1. An Autonomous Universe

The mind is a universe that determines itself spontaneously. It permanently works new ideas by recombining previous ideas. Locke proposed this first property in 1690. Biologists have since observed how it results from the operations of the brain. All parts of the brain can recombine ideas. Indeed, a brain is composed of cells called "neurons." Each neuron is connected by synaptic connections to other neurons. When a neuron generates a signal that it sends through the synapses, it stimulates other neurons that react in kind. Information travels from neuron to neuron. The activity of any neuron depend on other neurons.

The human brain is a massive network of permanently interacting fluxes of information. An adult brain is composed of about a hundred billion interacting cells. And there can be up to 10,000 synaptic connections per neuron.[1] These connections work out new combinations every moment, over a lifetime. The number of possible combinations is unfathomable. It also exceeds our current capacities of modelization. Many scientists have considered that explaining the human mind entirely would be forever impossible. The brain is often described as the most complex object known.

But it is also a very simple object. It is a single network. All neurons are connected. The mind is, as a result, a single process. All ideas are related. They are all associations of other ideas. All psychological events, all ideas, are produced by the same process of interference and recombination, either they are named as "ideas," "notions," "beliefs," "feelings," "fears," "desires" or "memories."[2] In the mind all events are connected. All must obey a common logic.

This logic also applies to all associations of ideas, including those who are influenced by external events, independent from the mind's own processes that stimulate the senses and generate sensorial messages that come to the mind. These perceptions in turn generate associations of ideas.

Experiments confirm our starting-point: all ideas can interfere with other ideas, whether perceptions or abstract ideas. Perceptions can interfere with other perceptions, either of the same sense or of different senses. They can also interfere with abstract ideas. And abstract ideas can interfere with each other.

Experiments reveal associations between perceptions of the same sense, for example, sight. An experiment was conducted during which persons were very briefly shown playing cards. They had to immediately name the colors: red or black. After a while, a red three of clubs was shown. In playing cards, the three of clubs is normally black. The red three of clubs was declared to be grey. This was the result of the association of the perception of a red three of clubs with the memory of a black three of clubs. This surprising result revealed a process that remained implicit in all other answers: the association of the perceptions with memories of previous perceptions.[3]

Experiments can also favor associations between perceptions by different senses. Gick and Derrick showed that tactile stimuli could interfere with auditory stimuli and alter the way they are understood. They applied without warning slight, inaudible air puffs on the right hand or on the neck. The word syllables that were played when air puffs were applied were more likely to be heard as aspirated. For example, "p" would be misheard as "b."[4]

Experiments can likewise favor associations between perceptions and abstract ideas. For example, Williams and Bargh showed that tactile stimuli could interfere with judgments about personality. Before the experiment explicitly began, the experimenter, seemingly struggling with an armful of folders, asked a volunteer to briefly hold a cup of coffee, either hot or iced. The volunteers then read a description of a person. Those who had held the warmer cup tended to consider that that person had a warmer personality.[5]

Experiments can finally favor associations between abstract ideas. For example, in another experiment, people were divided into two groups. During the first stage, people in the first group were asked to read an article that described airborne bacteria as a health hazard. The people in the second group did not see the article. During the second stage, all were asked to read an article about the history of the United States. It induced the idea that the nation was a kind of living organism through statements such as, "following the Civil War, the United States underwent a growth spurt." The people who had, during the first stage, read about dangerous bacteria were prone to making that association with US history. They were therefore more prone than the others to viewing immigration negatively, because immigration could be associated with dangerous bacteria.[6]

All experiments confirm our first principle: ideas of all types can be associated, perceptions as well as abstract ideas. It is a general property of the mind. The mind is a global process of associations of ideas.

2. A Spontaneous Logic

The mind spontaneously adopts a logic, always the same.

The mind is shaped by the external events it is exposed to, in a specific way. It anticipates them, based on its own experience. It associates its memories to the events it lives through. It imagines a course for the events to come that is inspired by those it experienced before. When it anticipates correctly, its perceptions do not conflict with the existing chain of ideas. They leave it intact. But when the mind does not anticipate correctly, perceptions do not match anticipations. They constitute new information. They interfere with the existing chain of event, disrupt it and recombine with it.

Experience therefore tends to facilitate correct anticipation of events. The formatting by new experiences was all the more intense when the mind was younger. At the extreme, when the mind was completely devoid of experience, any event could inform it. The mind in its totality was thus shaped by perceptions. It is the product of a life's experience. The process never ends. Events are too irregular. The mind can never anticipate all of them correctly.

Experiments confirm that past experiences can structure associations of ideas on the long term. For instance, when sensorial messages specifically evoke previous experiences, the mind can anticipate, by association, an outcome similar to the ones experienced in the past. Pavlov famously observed that a dog salivated simply upon hearing a bell which was usually rung just before meals. Both events had come to be associated in the dog's mind; the second one was eventually enough to trigger the reaction originally generated by the first one alone.[1]

Experiences also confirm that unanticipated events, but not anticipated ones, generate new information and reorganize the mind. This is observable through a peak in brain activity and a longer response. For example, infants were observed listening to a series of sounds. When they heard a series of standard sounds (like "ba, ba, ba, ba, ba"), brain imaging indicated that neuronal activity was at its most intense when the first sound in the series was perceived, and then diminished with each next sound. When the same infants heard a series of sounds with a deviant sound (like "ba, ba, ba, ba, go"), neuronal activity was at its most intense both when hearing the first sound and when hearing the deviant sound.[2] Infants also tended to look longer at unexpected events, a sign that these events were interfering with the normal train of thoughts and generating a specific response.[3]

The mind is shaped by the events its experiences. Since each life experience is unique, it is tempting to believe that each mind is essentially different from all others.

But the almost infinite variations in life experiences are of little consequence overall. Indeed all minds constantly treat the messages they receive in a similar way. As a result, they interpret the events in a similar, universal way. They acquire a similar logic out of their experiences.

At the core of the process are these disruptions, prompted by unanticipated events, that permanently modify the chain of ideas. They always do so in a similar way. Indeed, the mind always integrates the new information and reacts to it; thus, after a while, events are once again correctly anticipated and it always seems that the disruption ends.

For example, one is sitting and reading a book. The sudden ringing of a bell makes one jump in surprise. This is an unintended move and a departure from initial plans. However, it is followed by walking to the door and opening it. These are both successfully planned actions, as well as reactions to the unanticipated ringing and a permanent change of course from reading.

As a result, a sensorial disruption, that is an informative event, always leaves a memory comprised of three periods: in the first, perceptions match anticipations; in the second, perceptions do not match anticipations; in the third, perceptions once again match anticipations (Figure 1).

All informative events possess the same structure. None can disrupt this information. They can only reinforce it. It is therefore the fundamental structure of the mind, the universal structure that generates the universal logic of the human mind.

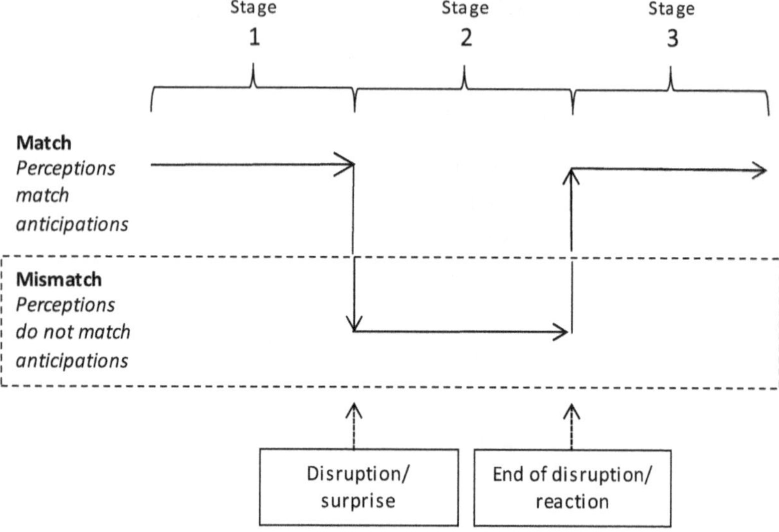

Figure 1. The fundamental structure of all informative events.

3. An Irresistible Drive

The mind is structured by the information is perceives. The most frequent information is also the simplest. It creates a fundamental structure. The mind cannot unlearn it, or reduce it to a simpler idea.

It can only reproduce it and build more complex ideas from it. As the most frequent idea, it is the most powerful vector of associations of ideas. It operates a superior pull on the mind. It is the most attractive idea. This fundamental idea, or fundamental structure, is therefore at the root of a universal worldview, a scenario that universally determines the desirability of any thought and action.

Our hypothesis is confirmed by the observation of the superior attractiveness of the ideas that are directly inspired by the fundamental structure. Since they are superiorly attractive, contradictory ideas cannot make them repellent, even when these contradictory ideas seem, on their own, quite compelling.

For instance, the idea of a disruption can be observed to be superiorly attractive. The fundamental structure includes a disruption. This fundamental experiment shapes all anticipations. The mind always anticipates another disruption. As its understanding of its world changes, the disruption that is imagined changes scale.

Toddlers love to destroy their creations and constructions, sand castles and the like; adolescents flock to violent disaster movies; adults are fascinated by natural catastrophes. Reports about tsunamis, volcanic eruptions and earthquakes regularly draw large audiences, in spite of the compassion one may feel for the victims and in spite of the sheer destruction of material assets.

If the human mind found pleasure primarily in capital accumulation (the "homo economicus" hypothesis), the sheer destruction of assets associated with natural catastrophes should make disruptions abhorrent. People would avoid such thoughts rather than be attracted by them. Likewise, if the human mind primarily relied on empathy, it would find natural catastrophes repellent. But these alternative hypotheses are falsified. Material rationality and empathy are not more attractive than a massive disruption of the natural order.

The mind always imagines a disruption to be temporary and abnormal; continuity and stability seem normal. As a consequence, our mind expects usual things and people to continue their existence even though our senses tell us that they disappear once they get out of reach. One is not surprised to find again a tree or a vase where one last observed it. The contrary would be surprising.

Any association of idea must follow the fundamental structure. It suggests both a stable order, a norm and an anomaly, a disruption of that order.

Any association of ideas is a binary association in which two ideas can be neatly distinguished as they are not symmetrical: one is expected to be repeated, as it corresponds to the order of things, while the other is not, as it is a disruption of that order.

Experiences confirmed that associations of ideas follow a binary structure. For instance, when asked whether people that are liked by good people are good or bad, the persons interviewed answered that they are good people. And when asked whether people disliked by bad people are good or bad, the persons interviewed also answer that they are good people. This result strikes anyone as common sense. It merely illustrates, it seems, a very straightforward concept, that the friend of your friend is your friend and that the enemy of your enemy is your friend too.[1] But if the mind's structure was not binary but unitary, any signal would simply reinforce any other signal and a person disliked by a bad person would be disliked, to a degree even superior.[2]

The mind always anticipates disruptions. And disruptions are always imagined to be temporary. They must end. Thus, the mind always anticipates the end of a disruption. And in the end, that anticipation always seems fulfilled.

The disruption has been unable to affect the correctness of that anticipation. In parallel to the disruption, something stayed untouched. The mind comes, by association, to imagine the existence of a continuous order that no disruption can affect, a "self," independent of all other events, capable of memorizing and anticipating events.

This "self" is also a "will." It anticipates the end of the disruption and that end is always realized, as if the self was capable of bending events to its will. The mind comes to imagine that there is a "will" operating on events to bring about the end of disruptions and restore order to the world.

Experiments confirm that the ideas of a self and a will, like the other structural ideas, result from past experiences. They are basically learned, and thus can be unlearned as well, at least temporarily, and then learned again.

Concerning the idea of one's will, the following was observed. The experiment conducted by Seligman and Maier consisted of submitting dogs to painful electrical shocks. Some dogs were harnessed and could not avoid the shocks while others could move freely. The dogs that were harnessed first tried to escape but could not avoid the shocks. After a while they did not seek to avoid them anymore. This state of passivity continued even when the dogs were detached and could again have moved away from the shocks. Instead, they just sat and whined. This result can only be explained by the fact that the dogs had un-learned that their will was effective. They knew they were unrestrained, and they knew that elsewhere they would not feel pain, like the unrestrained dogs that they could observe avoiding the shocks. However, they did not move anymore because, while they were restrained from moving, they had learned that wanting to avoid pain did not work. This conclusion is also supported by the fact that it was a reversible lesson: the dogs regained the capability to move in order to avoid pain after being forcibly moved away from shocks by the experimenters.[3]

Libet was able to record the electric impulses of the brain. He observed that the mental processes that command an action start before a person is able to acknowledge that they are willing to do that action. A person "knows" that they want to do something when they perceive their mind launching the action, rather than the reverse. [4] The will is therefore not what is usually imagined: a mental process independent of other mental processes, which it would somehow consciously precede and control. It is a representation produced by experience, like the other structural ideas, and like all other ideas.

The mind always anticipate another disruption. Most never happen except in imagination. However, the mind experiences them as if they were real. It witnesses itself imagining these disruptions, that is provoking them, willing them and fearing them at the same time.

To the mind, a disruption is therefore linked to a will, to a being that provokes it. The mind can only suspect that there are also wills behind those disruptions that it does not anticipate and to which it must react.

The mind constantly anticipates the presence of other beings, and constantly anticipates being surprised by their wills, bend on disruption.

This tendency to anticipate the presence of beings animated by the will to disrupt things has many specific, observable consequences.

First of all, the mind imagines such beings even it experiences a disruption, even when the disruption cannot be clearly traced to a source, let alone an incarnated being. For example, when an electric stimulation of the cortex provokes a muscular movement, the person interprets this as something "done to," not "happening" to them.[5]

Second, one can observe that when it experiences a disruption, the mind spontaneously imagines a will, and attributes it to the first source it can identify to the disruption. As a result, it can attribute it to people and objects alike.[6] Adults do it as spontaneously as infants and children.[7] This can for example be observed in everyday life when people involuntarily hit a door or a wall, get hurt and hit the object again, this time voluntarily, with the avowed desire to "punish" the culprit.

These actions can be observed because they obey the most rapid and powerful of associations of ideas. Otherwise, they would be repressed, prevented from developing. People would have time to analyze their impulse and admit they hit things that are inanimate and cannot possess the will that is imagined. But since these impulses obey the most powerful associations of ideas, they cannot be repressed by more powerful associations of ideas, and can be observed.

The fundamental character of the tendency to imagine wills and beings when confronted to a disruption is also confirmed by the tendency to imagine them even in relation to the meanest types of disruptions, like when confronted to new stimuli. For instance, people recognize faces in various types of objects when they first discover them. The "face in the moon" is probably one of the best known examples: the moon's patchwork of dark and light splotches is often likened to a human face with eyes, a nose and a mouth.

Experiments have shown people to recognize faces in objects such as plugs and tools as spontaneously and rapidly as they recognize real faces.[8] The capacity to distinguish inanimate objects from real faces is secondary in terms of speed and logic.

People develop that capacity only because they constantly anticipate being surprised by unanticipated events. And they constantly anticipate these events to be due to other wills, similar to their own, wills bend on disruption. Furthermore, they imagine these wills as incarnated beings. These wills are imagined to operate through a body, just like one's own will.

The spontaneous capacity endures throughout life. It is never completely repressed because it answers a most powerful tendency of the mind, one that is directly linked to the fundamental structure of the mind.

The mind always imagines that a disruption is anomalous, exceptional and unique. Therefore, in spite of their multiplication, all disruptions reinforce the idea of a unique disruption of the world's order. By association, the mind is irresistibly attracted to the idea of a single embodied, hidden will behind all disruptions, all evils: the Enemy. The mind always builds on the same core scenario: one world, one global order, disrupted by the Enemy, and one sees oneself, the greatest disrupter of disruptions that one knows, as the natural ender of the Enemy, the restorer of peace, the Hero of History (Figure 2).

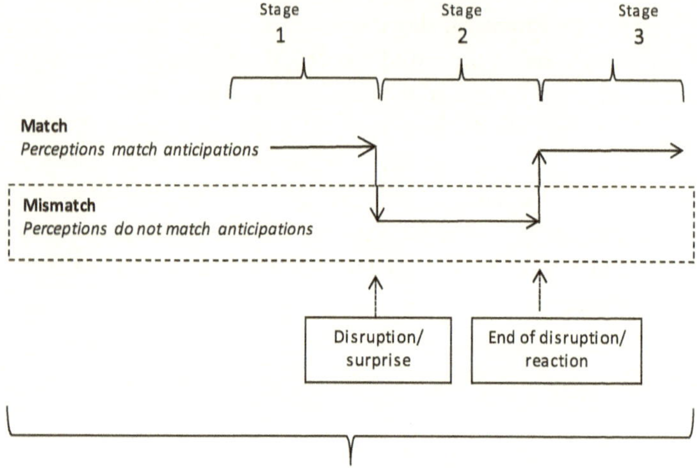

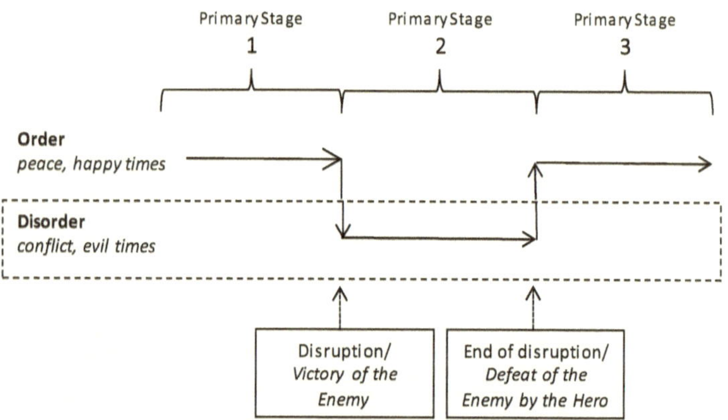

Figure 2. The reproduction of the fundamental structure. The structure of the memories of unanticipated and therefore informative events (1) is preserved and reproduced in the universal heroic scenario (2).

To be the Hero of History is the most attractive idea, the one which exercises the greatest pull on the mind. It is the supreme desire, the one which determines and organizes all other ideas and actions.

The simplest properties of the mind explain its universal structure. In spite of the considerable diversity of individual experiences, the mind always recombines the information it perceives into a heroic scenario. All events reinforce that vision of the world.

The attractiveness of an idea is proportional to its likeness to the heroic scenario. This can be illustrated by the following experiment: when asked to rate the desirability of a person's life, the people interviewed did not tend to rate it according to the cumulated number of happy years lived. They actually tended to rate it considerably better if a few happier years were added at the end of a rather miserable life. Likewise, they tended to rate a life considerably less favorably if a few less happy years were added at the end of a rather happy life. They did not rate her life twice as unhappy if the person lived twice as many unhappy years. Nor did they rate that life twice happier if the person lived twice as many happy years.[9] A happy end, relative to the rest of her life, was the most important criterion in judging her life desirable. Compared to it, the length of her life, and the accumulated years of happiness, seemed to have little influence on its global desirability.

These results are completely at odds with the classic theory in economics which predicts that they should prefer her to enjoy a maximum number of happy years.[10] But they are completely coherent with the hypothesis that the quest for heroism is the supreme desire. We think of life as a story and wish it to have above all a happy end.

The quest for heroism is the movement of the mind that no other can inhibit, limit or disrupt but that can disrupt and shape all others. It is the logic of the mind. And, as a consequence, it is the law of History: all events ultimately answer this supreme desire. All observations confirm this law. None falsifies it.

The universal structure of the mind can be further tested and confirmed through observations pertaining to its many necessary consequences, most notably the universal structure of narrative (Part II) and the universal dynamics in human activities (Part III and following).

*

This solves the fundamental problem in human science, a problem that dates from the first identification of the general properties of the mind by John Locke in *An Essay Concerning Human Understanding*.[11] Locke was indeed the first to propose a general theory of the human mind based on a mind operating by associations of ideas and organizing itself spontaneously from past experiences. And Locke considered that if each mind operated from its own original experience, it could not entertain "innate" ideas, especially universal ones.[12] Expressed in those terms, Locke's hypothesis seems self-evident.

Yet, from another point-of-view, Locke's explanation is clearly insufficient: if the mind is driven by a general dynamic of its own, it cannot just be educated in any direction as if it was a "tabula rasa" or an "empty cabinet."[13] Yet, Locke was not aware of this problem.

For instance, he correctly argued that the association of darkness and night with goblins and sprites must have been suggested to young children by nannies, parents, siblings or friends, but he never considered explaining why these ideas were appealing in the first place and why they were adopted and then nurtured for so long and with such intensity.

As a result of the dynamic of the mind, some ideas are clearly destined to be entertained while others are not. Having learned that fictional elves love trees does not make me expect to meet them when I walk in real woods. However, I am satisfied when, in fiction, I find elves with such qualities. From that point-of-view, Locke's explanation is obviously incomplete.

We must understand that Locke must have felt that his theory was a huge improvement upon the alternative theories of the day, and it was indeed in the context of his time, when all available examples of allegedly "universal" and "innate" ideas were explained away as being inspired by divine intervention and bear no relation with a structural explanation of the mind.

The most famous of the works that upheld Locke's hypotheses during the following decades is David Hume's *Treatise on Human Nature*. Hume clearly observed cases of ideas that, if we follow his own account, have all the appearances of being universal. They are so characteristic of the fundamental workings of the mind that Hume uses them as case studies. For instance, he noted that people imagine that objects have a continuous existence, although our senses tell us that they disappear when they are not perceived.[14] He also observed that all people imagine a "self," a personal identity.[15] Finally, he remarked that people believe that the whole universe is a single entity.[16] These idea are indeed universal, and due to the structure of the mind.

Yet, like Locke, Hume simply rejected innate ideas.[17] The problem that was to become so central for human science in the next centuries must have seemed a secondary one at the time, the sort of difficulty that would sooner or later be reconciled with the principles of Locke. And indeed, it is now, three centuries later, solved and explained in accordance with the principle of an autonomous mind that Locke first upheld, if at the cost of his second principle, that excluded universal ideas.

4. An Unspeakable Desire

The quest for heroism is the universal logic of the human mind. But it is extremely well concealed from those it governs. To be the Hero of History may be the supreme desire. But no one ever admits it. In fact, no one is even conscious of it. This seems paradoxical. Yet, it is only logical.

The first person to which I presented this general theory to simply commented: "Well, for my part, I do not feel like I want to be the Hero of History."

We feel conscious of our thinking. We have a sense of a self. We feel we are in control of our own actions. It seems that for all but a few moments of surprises, and rare bouts of illness and delirium, we are aware of what is going on. Our mind gives us little room to envisage that it could all be an illusion. On the contrary: it has us to think we are in touch with reality. Even when we dream, we feel like it is real; the more intense the dream the more we are taken aback when we wake up. But then, we can easily dismiss it as a dream, or a nightmare, a kind of anomaly. We cannot even imagine that we are unaware of the innermost logic of our mind.

We cannot know either from our own personal experiences that we desire above all to be the Hero of History. We cannot understand it is a desire, let alone the supreme one. We recognize desires because they vary in intensity. They can be resisted and sometimes renounced altogether. They can thus be attributed to one's own mind. However, the quest for heroism cannot be recognized as an impulse of our mind. It entirely shapes the vision we have of the world and our understanding of the role we have to play. It does not vary and cannot be resisted. We think the world is just that way.

Furthermore, it is not possible to observe the one phenomenon that would seem the most logical and the most straightforward consequence of the quest for heroism: that everyone claims they are indeed the Hero.

In fact, not everyone denies being the Hero of History. Young children do not. Of course, they do not use these precise words. They do not say, "I want to be the Hero of History." This expression denotes our generalization of countless heroic scenarios which are each quite specific. But children are not ashamed to share with their companions and caretakers fantasies and scenarios where they, and no one else, play the heroic role.

For example, my four-year-old son very seriously told me on a weekend walk at the park: "I will defend you and Mommy." I spontaneously thought of flies and spiders, although I should have known better. When I asked him "what will you be fighting against?" he replied to my surprise and amusement, "dragons." He does not share such ideas anymore. He has grown up. At the age of ten, I can still hear him playing imaginary scenarios. But now he requires privacy. He does it only when alone in his room.

People learn to suppress stories or arguments that would suggest they are special and better. They learn to do so during childhood.

When I was three years old, I was invited by neighbors to a picnic. I played with their son who was about the same age and it seems I must have repeated many times, "I am the *tief*" because I could not pronounce correctly "I am the chief." My friend did not seem to mind. After all, at that age children usually just play along and find inspiration in one another's moves without looking for a very complex, foolproof scenario. I may have been the chief and he could have been the chief too. But my friend's parents minded what I said and they decided it was noticeable enough to repeat it to my parents in the evening when we came back. They actually took care to repeat it exactly the way I said it: "I am the *tief*." And my parents must have found it amusing too, because the memory endured for many years afterwards.

My friend's parents would not have noticed if it had not annoyed them somehow. They were worried that their son was too shy, not self-assured enough. They feared that so eagerly claiming I was the *tief* was not helping. Mocking me gently was their way of establishing a limit.

So it is during childhood that people learn to suppress heroic ideas. They continue to do so throughout adulthood. Very few people suggest they could be the Hero of History because they have learned no one else would support such a claim. They may not understand that each one, like themselves, would rather claim the role for themselves. But they know that anyone would call it pure madness if someone else was expressing such ideas. One would be left isolated, ridiculed and pitied. Upon realizing this, almost everyone keeps to oneself any thought of being an extraordinary being.

Adults occasionally express such ideas nonetheless, when their own prolonged isolation has made them lose a sense of what could be appropriately shared. For example, patients in a psychiatric hospital may be open about their own unique destiny in ways that most people are not. They may argue for months with one another about which one is the real Christ.[1]

Most adults, however, never express such thoughts. In fact, they are not even conscious of nurturing them. They have repressed the expression of their heroic dreams. They have come to admit that only what is confirmed by companions is true and companions would never confirm such ideas.

Personal fantasies gradually lose their appeal. In secret, adolescents still nurture the idea that one day all others will have no choice but to recognize their special qualities. Most adults have become comfortable with admitting, even to themselves, that this is neither reasonable nor realistic. If asked, they would say that of course they do not desire to be a hero, let alone the Hero of History.

The repression of the desire to claim being the Hero of History is in itself a sign of the presence and power of the supreme desire. Unaware of it, people continue to be inspired by a heroic worldview. Even if they deny it, they will always be supremely attracted by it. A desire needs not be conscious to endure. Even repressed, the innermost logic of the mind is still detectable by its specific consequences. The quest for heroism can be observed through the universal structure of narratives and the universal dynamics in human activities.

II

To be the Hero of History

The quest for heroism is the movement of the mind that no other can impair. Its consequences can be observed everywhere in human activity.

It generates first of all a universal worldview that can be observed in the universal structure of the narratives that people invent and pass on. These narratives are all based on the heroic scenario; they contain fundamental and universal notions that never vary and do not depend on any specific circumstances to be attractive. These elements can be found in historical accounts like in fiction: a unique History, a unique World, a unique Hero and a unique, intimate Enemy. Together, they compose the universal heroic scenario.

As a result, fiction and historical narratives universally share the same structure: three primary stages and two disruptive events set in an immutable sequential order: first, the peaceful stage which ends when it is disrupted by the Enemy; second, evil times dominated by the Enemy; and finally, the destruction of the Enemy by the Hero and the restoration of peace and order to the world.

However, by contrast with fiction, historical accounts are bound to leave open the position of the Hero, so that both the author and the reader could be that person. Indeed, each one desires above all to be the Hero of History. No one would accept that someone else occupies that position. Historical accounts in which authors claim to be the Hero are not shared and passed on. But since each one desires to be the Hero, attractive narratives must make a convincing case that the time of decisive action against the Enemy is near. One seeks to share a sense of danger looming and a call to action (*5 – A Universal Scenario*).

Fiction and historical narratives all contain references to a unique world. Fictional worlds may resemble the real one, but the more closely they evoke it, the more they have to be explicitly distinguished from it. In the author's as well as in the reader's mind, there can implicitly be only one real history and only one real world, because there is only one real Enemy and one real Hero. Thus, fiction evokes and reinforces the fundamental notions of the heroic scenario. It is a source of inspiration for action (*6 – A Unique History*).

The desire to be the Hero of History exists since childhood and never disappears. The role adults desire in national history is simply a more complex version of the childish heroic scenario related to the family circle. And the adults continue to be inspired by childish desires (*7 – A Unique Goal, from Childhood On*).

Indeed, fiction and historical narratives equally contain references to an intimate Enemy, a hidden being, uniquely malevolent and dangerous, who wants to upset the world order and dominate all things. In fiction, only the Hero seems to have a special, intimate knowledge of the Enemy's presence. In reality, each one feels that they have a deep, intimate connection with the danger, one that they cannot detect to the same extent in other people, because childish desires related to the sole family circle are not discussed anymore between adults, although they are still present to the mind. This sense of uniqueness reinforces the notion of being the Chosen One, called to action by a special destiny (*8 – A Unique, Intimate Enemy*).

5. A Universal Scenario

Fictional or historical, the stories that people pass on are all inspired by a universal heroic scenario, with three primary stages and two disruptive events set in an immutable sequential order (Figure 3). First is the original golden age, a state of peace and order which is destroyed by the victory of the Enemy (Primary Stage 1). It is followed by evil times (Primary Stage 2). Finally, the victory of the Hero and the destruction of the Enemy restore the golden age (Primary stage 3).

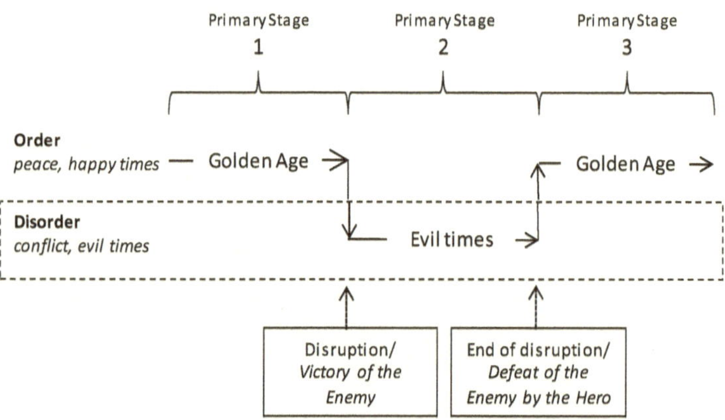

Figure 3. The universal heroic scenario, universal structure of narratives.

Each narrative must contain all three primary stages. But each of them can appear only once, as there can be only one destruction of the golden age and only one defeat of the Enemy. Indeed, there is only one Enemy and only one Hero.

Many other stages can be added between the destruction of the golden age and its restoration; as opposed to the three primary stages, their number and sequential order are variable. Creativity has limits, though: facts incompatible with the heroic scenario are ignored. For example, narratives never dwell on excessive use of violence by the heroes and their companions; they never cast their adversaries as victims. The victims of the Enemy cannot be the authors of misdeeds equivalent to those of the Enemy. He alone is the ultimate source of evil; his destruction ends evil forever.

This universal structure can be illustrated by historical accounts as well as fictional stories such as fairy tales. There is, however, one constant difference between the two types of stories: the defeat of the Enemy and the return of the golden age always happen in a tale, but these events are only anticipated in the historical accounts that are shared and passed on. In consequence, while the identities of fictional heroes are always known, the identity of the Hero of History has yet to be revealed.

Here are two examples of tales and two examples of historical accounts in which the three primary stages can be easily recognized.

The first example is "Hansel and Gretel," one of the Grimm Brothers' tales.[1] At the beginning, the two children live happily with their parents (original golden age). But a great famine settles over the land and the mother dies. The father, depressed, marries a woman that does not love the children. The stepmother persuades the father to abandon Hansel and Gretel deep in the woods, so that they will not come back and will not have to be nourished anymore. The father eventually consents, and the children get lost. Wandering in the woods, they discover a house made of cakes and sweets, and a very old woman invites them inside. The witch makes Hansel a prisoner. She fattens him and plans to eat him. The children vainly try to escape (evil times). As the witch prepares to cook Hansel, Gretel manages to push her by surprise into the hot oven where she burns (destruction of evil). Free at last, the children plunder the riches of the witch and find their way back home where their father greets them with joy. The stepmother is dead. He realizes how much he missed his children and regrets having abandoned them. They all live happily ever after (final golden age).

Depending on the version of the tale, many other sequences are added. For example, Hansel and Gretel's father and stepmother usually try several times in vain to abandon the children in the woods. The first time, Hansel, who has overheard their plans, collects white pebbles, puts them in his pocket and drops them along the road. To return home, the two children simply follow the pebbles. The next time, suspecting a trick, the father locks the children in during the night and Hansel cannot collect pebbles. He uses white bread crumbs instead, but the birds eat them before he can trace his way home, and the children get lost. These additional parts are not necessary to the tale and could be omitted, contrary to the three primary stages.

"Ali Baba and the Forty Thieves," one of the tales from *One Thousand and One Nights,* is another famous example of a story in which the three primary stages are easily recognized.[2] Ali Baba is a poor merchant who lives with his family in a small town in Persia (original golden age). One day, in the countryside, he catches sight of a group of thieves. He follows them to their treasure trove, a cave, and while there, he overhears the password, "open sesame," which magically opens the cave. Ali Baba helps himself to the riches. However, his newfound wealth attracts too much attention. His jealous brother discovers his secret and breaks into the cave. Alas, he is caught by the thieves who kill him and leave his body in the cave. Ali Baba discovers his dead brother and buries him, but removing the body from the cave reveals his existence to the thieves. They now seek by all means to kill him (evil times). He is saved by his cunning servant, Morgiana. Time and again, she foils the thieves' plans until all forty thieves are dead (destruction of evil). This shows Ali Baba that life and family are more valuable than gold. He eventually marries his nephew to Morgiana in great pomp (final golden age).

Again, many sequences are usually added before the final destruction of evil. The forty thieves use several disguises in efforts to approach Ali Baba, kill him, and recover their gold. Each time, Morgiana recognizes them. In the end, they decide to hide in jars, and Morgiana pours boiling oil in the jars, killing all thieves – except for their chief whom she kills last.

Developments and possible consequences incompatible with the heroic scenario are omitted. For instance, in both "Ali Baba" and "Hansel and Gretel," the villains die gruesome deaths at the hands of the heroes. But that does not turn them into victims and the heroes into malevolent people. Their end is implicitly deemed justified.

The three primary sequences of the heroic scenario can also be observed in historical accounts. For example, at the turn of the twentieth century, the French government promoted a textbook of the history of France which argued that France had once been a country named Gaul, with natural borders on the Pyrenees, the Alps, the Atlantic, the Mediterranean and, most importantly, on the Rhine River. Thanks to the Romans, Gaul had been unified, pacified and civilized (original golden age). But barbaric German invaders had swept the country during the fifth century and forced the Gauls, renamed French, to ploy under the yoke of despotic rulers (destruction of the golden age). The people of France, under their kings, had to fight through centuries to recover their lost freedom and be united again.

The textbook was entirely designed to suggest that the liberation of Gaul was an unfinished struggle and that the millennial war against the German hereditary Enemy demanded a final victory which would free the part of Gaul still occupied by Germany (anticipated destruction of the Enemy and restoration of the golden age).[3]

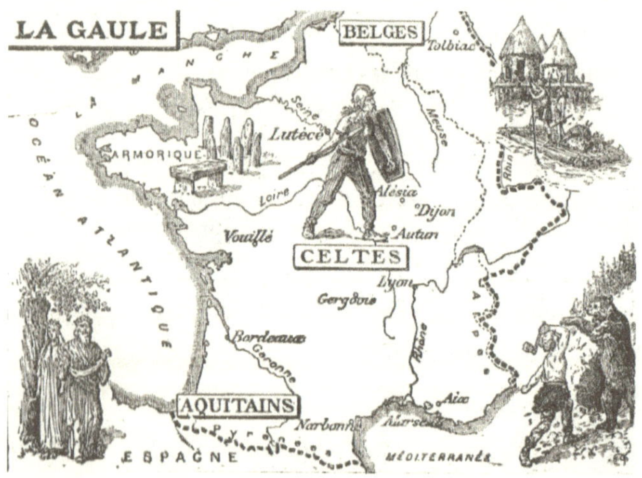

Figure 4: Ancestral Gaul with its borders (heavy dashes) and those of 1900 France (dashes).

For instance, the book opened with a map that compared 1900 France and Ancestral Gaul. The borders were identical except for the eastern part of Gaul which was occupied by Germany. In the middle of the map, a Gaulish warrior faced Germany (Figure 4).[4]

Facts that were incompatible with the heroic scenario were ignored, such as those suggesting that the Gauls were never a united people or those indicating how much the Germanic presence shaped a distinct French language and culture.

Another example is a history of the Irish nation, published in 1965. Like similar contemporary publications, it indicated that the Irish arrived in Ireland around 500 BCE. They seemed to have inhabited a prosperous country for centuries (golden age). They repelled all invasions until the English defeated them in the twelfth century and colonized the island. These early English conquerors in turn largely adopted Irish customs and language, but later English attacks overwhelmed them and eventually suppressed all liberties, reducing the Irish to extreme poverty and famine, and forcing them to adopt English ways or to emigrate (destruction of the golden age). Eventually, after "seven hundred years of oppression,"[5] the remaining Irish rose victoriously against the English and liberated the South of Ireland, where they proclaimed an independent Irish Republic.

However, this happy ending could only be a provisory one. It was only a partial reversal of the situation. The English still occupied the North of Ireland while English remained the common language in the South, which was also heavily dependent on English trade. The situation in 1965 thus opened several directions for activist groups: a re-conquest of the North, the replacement of English by Irish as the everyday language, an autarchic economy, or at least one less dependent on England, etc. All these policies could be seen as necessary for the completion of the struggle for independence, and were indeed implemented with various degrees of success (anticipated final rising against the Enemy and restoration of the golden age).[6]

Once again, facts incompatible with the heroic scenario tended to be ignored. The author noted that the Irish arrived in Ireland at the earliest in 500 BCE, when the island was already populated. But he did not deduce that the Irish were invaders like the later Vikings or the English. He did not discuss either whether the Irish exterminated previous cultures and languages or merely assimilated parts of them, as did later invaders. Like other Irish historians, he denounced English oppression, and claimed that the Irish were the legitimate inhabitants of Ireland. Irish was, therefore, their rightful national language and culture.

Like tales, historical narratives are based on three primary stages: an original golden age, its destruction by the Enemy followed by evil times, and the final restoration of the golden age that follows the destruction of the Enemy. However, historical narratives differ from fictional ones in that they only anticipate the final victory over the Enemy and the return of the golden age.

The ends of major conflicts are particularly marked by the anticipation of an end of times and a return to a golden age.

For example, in 1918, when a coalition led by France, Britain and the United States eventually won the war against Germany and its allies, the war (later to be named World War I) was nicknamed "the Last War" ("La Der des Ders"). Likewise, when Octavianus was about to bring an end to the Roman civil wars, Virgil mused about a return of the "golden age." On December 25, 1991, the President of the United States, George

Bush, declared that the Cold War was over. The next year, Francis Fukuyama published *The End of History*, speculating that the world was now forever in an era of peace dominated by the US and free-market policies.[7]

*

The discovery of the universal structure of stories, and notably of their three primary stages, started more than a century ago with the analysis of the structure of tales and legends. Tales are often mocked because of their predictability; it is well known that the hero always survives to triumph in the end; this idea made intuitive that all tales follow a common structure.

Vladimir Propp was a precursor. In 1928 he published an analysis of one-hundred Russian fairy tales. He had found that eight character types, which he named "spheres of action," were very frequent: the aggressor or the villain, the princess and her father, the king, the hero that vanquishes the villain, the false hero, the dispatcher that sends the hero on his mission, the helper, and the donor.[8] According to Propp, the reader follows these characters through different types of stages, which he named "functions." Propp distinguished thirty-one different stages: the estrangement, the interdiction, the transgression, and so on. Propp remarked that they were not ordered rigidly; some stages could be missing, and others could be repeated.[9] However, two stages were always present: the misdeed and the following reparation, also named the loss and the redemption when the villain was not evident.[10]

Propp had indeed discovered the two disruptive events that separate the three primary stages of the narrative. Brémond and Barthes recognized these invariants and labelled them a "structure" and a "narrative cycle."[11] Ricoeur added that the response is actually brought about by a "hero" fighting evil and endowed with certain qualities that set them apart from the rest of the community.[12] These elements are similar to those independently identified by Campbell in relation to fantasy fiction works.[13]

Rank was the first to conjecture that a universal structure of narratives would necessarily imply a universal structure of the human mind.[14] His theory was later endorsed by Lévi-Strauss[15] and Barthes.[16]

However, the identification of the universal structure of the human mind was hindered by a second hypothesis, formulated in Aristotle[17] and unquestioned since, even by Barthes,[18] that narratives other than fiction (i.e. historical accounts), cannot, contrary to fiction, have a common structure.

It appears, with hindsight, that success was hindered by the very structure the researchers sought to uncover. Fictional stories are spontaneously compared. The structure common to all tales is therefore quite intuitive. However, tales are also spontaneously opposed to historical accounts, which present themselves, on the contrary, as series of unique events. A structure of historical accounts is therefore not intuitive. The cause of the distinction is deeply rooted into the structure of the mind: if History was not unique, the universe, the Enemy and the Hero, could not be unique either.

The theory of the difference between fiction and history can be traced back to Aristotle, who proposed the example of Homer to illustrate the difference. Homer's genius, according to Aristotle, lay in his ability to compose an epic story about the Trojan War by selecting specific events from the chronological events recorded, and arranging them so as to give them a uniquely tragic and epic dimension. This radical distinction

74

between fiction and historical accounts was unnecessary. Aristotle overlooked that the unity of plot observable in Homer was probably inspired by historical accounts which similarly isolated the Trojan War as a dramatic story. They probably established the origins and causes of the war, emphasized the key events of the conflict, and explained how one side finally prevailed upon the other.

Aristotle's radical distinction between fiction and history was actually quite influential in scientific circles. As a consequence, the sequential structure of national histories has not attracted as much attention as that of the tales. Anthony Smith pioneered the field nonetheless and observed striking similarities between national histories.[19] He noted that they often share similar "myths": nation birth myths, "a Myth of Temporal Origins" or "When We Were Begotten," "a Myth of Ancestry" or "Who Begot Us and How We Developed," and also "a Myth of the Heroic Age" or "How We Were Freed and Became Glorious," "a Myth of Regeneration" or "How to Restore the Golden Age and Renew Our Community as in the Days of Old," etc. Smith also observed that a "significant other" can "serve as a traditional enemy" and reconcile antagonistic traditions, but he did not give that figure a central role nor did he link the different myths he analyzed. He did not draw a parallel with the structure of tales. To recognize the same sequential structure in tales and historical accounts was certainly fraught with difficulties.

Historical accounts must partly differ from fiction in the expression of the structure. First, historical accounts usually develop on average the first sequence, the origins, much more than fiction. Competition between historians generates considerable attention to the beginnings of times because they define by contrast evils committed later and also who is best placed to lead the fight against the Enemy and restore the natural order. By contrast, authors of fiction do not on average pay as much attention to initial circumstances, since no one usually challenges the credentials of their hero. Children's tales are typically being characterized by the well-known stereotypical opening and final sentences – "Once upon a time" and "they lived happily ever after."

Second, historical accounts do not usually devote much space to the anticipation of the last stage, the destruction of evil, because the more specific the authors are about that part, the more they seem to claim for themselves some heroic role. No one would accept to disseminate such a narrative. Third, as a consequence, hoping to help the dissemination of their work, historians also tend to refer explicitly or implicitly to other partial accounts by colleagues or companions. It is difficult to reconstruct the full meaning of any of these partial accounts if one does not belong to the circle of the authors.

6. A Unique History

The quest for heroism, our desire to become the Hero of History, shapes our vision of the world. It makes people imagine a heroic scenario: a unique reality, a unique history in a unique world, our "universe." This is necessary to allow thinking that the Enemy is unique and that his destruction will bring an end to all evils.

Fiction, like historical accounts, is attractive only in so far as it evokes the heroic scenario. But fiction is attractive only when history is frustrating, when circumstances seem inadequate to act heroically, when the audience must bid their time. It is a world of substitution but not a world that cannot be fully substituted to reality nonetheless, for no one renounces to be the real Hero.

Thus, fiction must never be confused with reality. It is essential that the reader be left with no doubt that reality is unique. The more a fictional world resembles reality, the more precisely distinguished from reality it must be.

The "villain" of the tale, the simplest type of fiction, is far from a perfect Enemy. He is not hidden but, on the contrary, is easily identifiable. The conflict that opposes him to the hero is little justified, making it look more like a private question than a cause that needs the concern of a whole world. For an adult reader in particular, it is an unattractive figure of the Enemy, which is translated into a diminishing name: the "villain." Indeed, tales are often deemed more interesting for children who have not yet acquired a complex vision of the world in which they live.

Complex worlds evoke better the Enemy, at least in the eyes of an adult audience. A complex world, with detailed and coherent geographical, social, legal and chronological aspects, allows the Enemy to appear unique in contrast to the diversity of his opponents. Only in a complex world is it possible to imagine that the Enemy can successfully hide himself. Only there can he be an all-threatening character that forces all his opponents to forget their rivalries and enmities to fight him.

This sort of fiction is well illustrated by J.R.R. Tolkien's *The Lord of the Rings*.[1] In the world of Middle-earth, all people are threatened by one evil will, Sauron, who is often simply called "the Enemy." All evil beings bend to his will, even the most powerful, such as the wizard Saruman. Sauron has no body and no face. He lives concealed in the remote realm of Mordor. His Ring is mysteriously his most powerful instrument and his only embodiment; it is spoken of as "the One Ring" or "the Unique." To destroy Sauron means to destroy the Ring. The world in which the story takes place, Middle-earth, is a very detailed one, with very detailed geography, chronology, and even linguistics. All inhabitants of Middle-earth eventually realize that they must either submit to Sauron or unite their forces to resist him.

For these reasons, *The Lord of the Rings* appears much less like a simple fairy tale than *The Hobbit*, which it is nonetheless supposed to prolong. *The Hobbit* [2] was also illustrated by a map, but the plot only concerned the successive places visited by the hero, Bilbo, not a whole world. Bilbo met many dangerous situations: trolls, orcs, Gollum, a dragon, and orcs again… but there was no central threat. The Ring that was designed to become so central and threatening in *The Lord of the Rings* is nothing more than a magical ring that makes its bearer invisible. Adversaries never submit to a single will. As a result, the scenario evokes a tale in spite of its length and complexity. In that respect, the recent films in Peter Jackson's trilogy *The Hobbit*[3] depart from Tolkien's book. They give Sauron a central role, making the quest of Bilbo and his dwarf companions more important for the whole of Middle-earth than Tolkien initially suggested. This was, of course, perceived to be necessary to captivate the same adult audience that had been attracted to Peter Jackson's *The Lord of the Rings*.

Complex worlds produce more attractive manifestations of the Enemy. As a consequence, the more complex the description of the imaginary world, the more precisely distinguished from the accepted reality it has to be. Like Middle-earth in the *Lord of the Rings*, such worlds usually possess a distinct name, specific creatures and a particular kind of magic that makes the particular laws of our world irrelevant. By contrast, simple tales typically do not need to be very specific and usually start with vague formulas such as "a long time ago, far, far away…" which pretend to leave to the reader whether they belong to the real world or to an imaginary one.

Some cases might be misleading. For example, the universe of *Star Wars* is a rather complex one, but the introductory sentence looks like that of a tale:

"A long time ago, in a galaxy far, far away…"[4]

A single word, "galaxy," actually makes its world immediately much more specific than in most other tales. Conversely, tales that may seem at first glance specifically located may not be so. For example, in *The One Thousand and One Nights,* the story of Aladdin is supposed to take place in "China."

However, that country has little in common with real China. "China" simply designates a place where the readers have never been: a land far, far away from medieval Arabia and Persia where the story was composed.[5]

Complex imaginary worlds need to be set at a clear distance from the accepted reality, and they need to be moved further away as the known world expands. As the great discoverers, such as Thomas Cook, had left almost no place on the surface of Earth unvisited, Jules Verne's nineteenth-century imaginary worlds were placed "20,000 leagues under the sea,"[6] in the air or far under the Earth's surface.

In the twentieth century, as these spaces were being explored, science-fiction had to move to the outer space. But even there, the border between what is known and ignored changed. The first exoplanets were discovered in 1995 between the production of the first and second *Star Wars* trilogies, which took place respectively in 1977-1983 and 1999-2005. This discovery has narrowed the distance between imaginary extraterrestrial worlds and real ones. The script writers felt they had to react somehow to this change. It was therefore evoked by Qui-Gon Jinn in *The Phantom Menace*, the first episode of the second trilogy.[7] The Jedi explained to the young Anakin Skywalker that most stars are indeed orbited by planets. This point was left unanswered in the first trilogy.

Fiction and historical narratives all contain references to a unique world. Fictional worlds may resemble the real one, but the more closely they evoke it, the more they have to be explicitly distinguished from it. Complex fictional worlds must be explicitly distinguished from reality in order to preserve the idea of a single reality.

In reverse, historical accounts may also be declared fictional when they evoke too closely the idea that the Enemy could have already been defeated. This was what happened to the story of the Minotaur. The monster, half-bull half-man, was supposed to have lived hidden in the Labyrinth, in Crete. Each year, the Athenians had to send seven young men and seven young women as a tribute to the Minotaur who ate them. According to the story, one day, Theseus, the son of the King of Athens, entered the Labyrinth, killed the monster, and freed his people from the tribute.[8] The hidden monster, whose death sufficed to end all sufferings, is a typical evocation of the Enemy. This is why ancient and modern historians always classified the episode as legendary, in spite of its inclusion in a historical account, the history of Athens. Whether the Minotaur was biologically possible is hardly ever discussed; historians usually consider as their duty to seek and find the real and forgotten meaning behind what they automatically classify as a legend. They deduce from it that Athens was a subject of a Cretan City, usually identified with the labyrinthic Palace of Knossos.

In the author's as well as in the reader's mind, there can implicitly be only one real history and one real world, because there is only one real enemy and one real hero. Thus, fiction is not the negation or the renouncement to the quest for heroism. It evokes and reinforces the fundamental notions of the heroic scenario. In the end, it is a call for action in reality.

As a consequence, the attractiveness of fictional worlds reveals itself only when real action seems frustrated. For example, Gandalf, one of the main characters of *The Lord of the Rings*, was evoked by Vietnam War protesters. "Gandalf for President" was one of their slogans to signify their deep disillusionment with US President Lyndon B. Johnson.

Fiction is always subordinated to reality. When real action becomes attractive, fiction becomes dull. This could be observed in the case of EverQuest, a massive multi-player online role-playing game in the early 2000s. Players classically used an avatar, a personal, customized character through which they could permanently interact with other avatars. They played in the world of Norrath, which was extensively mapped and detailed, complete with cities such as Freeport and Qeynos, a currency, the platina, myths and legends, and various species: rivers, gods, wizards, giants, trolls, frogs…

The game had a reputation for being extremely addictive. Players acknowledged that life on Norrath was more thrilling than real life. It was so attractive that it generated real business, well beyond the plans of the game creators. For example, players sold and exchanged avatars and goods on platforms run by firms not controlled by the game owners, Sony and Verant, who vainly sought to prohibit the practice. Acts committed by avatars also led to real protests. For example, a rape that occurred on Norrath led a law professor to demand sanctions.

However, real politics were still capable of interfering with the game. Rules were contested, such as those prohibiting same-sex marriages. This was a theme of electoral campaigns in many countries at that time, including in the United States. Eventually, during Gulf War II, in 2003, avatars took sides for or against the US invasion of Iraq. A player recalled that "the external world took over. Norrath seemed dull."[9]

The attractiveness of fiction always depends on reality and the immediate possibilities it seems to offer to satisfy our chief desire, to be the unique Hero of History.

*

Propp left over one enigma. When he analyzed one-hundred Russian tales, he recognized a "villain" only in a majority of them. In the rest he saw no villain at all. He considered that the hero had only to accomplish a "difficult task."[10] Does it mean that the structure of tales is not a universal one? It is actually very likely that the *difficult-task-sort-of* tale may just be a tale in which the evil being is so diminished that it is difficult to recognize him at all as a central figure.

The difficulty in identifying the villain may be illustrated by a famous tale, Charles Perrault's *Puss in Boots*.[11] The feline hero only meets a truly dangerous situation during the final sequence, as he conquers for his master a castle from an ogre. On the one hand, it is difficult to consider the ogre as a central figure in the tale: he plays no role except in that sequence. He is an isolated image of evil and means no threat to the rest of the realm. On the other hand, he is the only truly dangerous character in the tale, and a happy ending typical of fairy tales immediately follows his death: the master of *Puss in Boots* marries the princess and the cat lives in the castle happily ever after. Thus, the ogre plays a part that is indeed evocative of the "villain" of the tale; but it is one that is so downplayed that the conquest of his castle may simply be classified as a "difficult task."

To a lesser degree, the same difficulty arises in the tale of "Hansel and Gretel." It is possible to classify this story as a difficult-task-sort-of tale because there is no unique central evil, but rather a succession of villains that require the children to find different solutions to survive. First, the parents maneuver to lose the children in the woods. The children are forced to implement different counter-maneuvers to find their way back home. The children eventually get lost nonetheless and become prisoners of a witch. They develop various tactics to avoid being eaten and finally resort to radical action to get rid of her. Who really is the villain? The father who abandoned them, the stepmother who persuaded him to do so, or the witch who tried to cook and eat them? The witch is doubtlessly the most convincing candidate; she is the only one to be actually destroyed by the heroes. Moreover, difficulties wither away immediately after her death. The children live happily ever after with their father. The manipulative stepmother who wanted the children abandoned is not such a good candidate. Some authors indicate that she died before the end of the story and others that she starved to death. Some simply seem to have forgotten her; she simply vanishes from the end of the tale. Of course, with a little imagination, one could solve the difficulty and imagine that the stepmother actually was the witch. After all, in *Snow White and the Seven Dwarfs*, the jealous stepmother is also the witch that poisons Snow White, at least in the version inspired by the Grimm Brothers' tales[12] and produced by the Walt Disney Studios.[13] This scenario has the advantage of producing a central, easily identifiable villain. But the witch would still be classified as a villain, not as a convincing figure of the Enemy. Indeed, by destroying the villain, the heroes liberate only themselves, not the whole world.

"Tales" – as in "fairy tales" or "children's tales" – are the type of narrative that has been the most frequently studied to identify a common structure. It is the literary genre that appears the most stereotyped and that seems the most distinguished from our unique history.

The heroic scenario can be more difficult to recognize in other types of fiction, like popular or high literature, because they give the readers cause to believe they are more realistic than tales. An important difference between popular fiction, like the James Bond series, and tales, are the multiple references to contemporary reality in the James Bond series: the hero is a British Cold War secret agent who travels in real countries, enjoys cocktails, cars and beautiful women, etc. Multiple details are sown into the narrative to give it a semblance of realism,[14] although the glamorous and brutal reality of James Bond was of course to remain forever inaccessible to his audience.

But all types of fiction play with the same structure. This can be revealed by the risk that all fiction equally faces when becoming too stereotyped and repetitive: they tend to lose their appeal, like tales do from the point of view of adults. For example, the James Bond novels and film series always opposed the hero, James Bond, to an evil person bent on world domination. The continuation of Bond's adventures throughout several books and movies, where the evil characters ended up killed one after another, compromised the unity of evil and diminished as a result the danger that each new evil character incarnated. This diminution must have been felt by the author and screenwriters. They tried to reinforce a sense of unity in evil by revealing that all the bad guys actually belonged to a single secret organization bent on world domination, appropriately named "Specter."

It might seem then that the real difference is between tales and popular fiction on the one hand, and high literature on the other. But then again, this would be an illusion. High literature relies on the literary capital of its public, and especially on their knowledge of simpler works, like tales and popular fiction. They are a necessary reference in works that deliberately stage antiheroes, banal heroes or everyday heroes who are not to save the world, their friends or even able to maintain a happy relationship with anyone.

Such fiction cannot ignore the notions at the core of the heroic scenario; on the contrary, it builds upon them. One need only think about *Don Quixote*, the model of the genre. The book, which presents itself as written to mock chivalry books, is full of literary references. It even mentions chivalrous adventures such as those of Amadis de Gaule.[15] In fact, the central sequences are only about the repeated failure of the main character to become the hero. Only the reader's – perhaps foolish – hope of a different outcome can explain the comic or pathetic effect.[16]

High literature works can be considered as a more complex play with the same fundamental structure. It is not one that could ignore the structure. This is of course why it is often impossible to distinguish popular fiction from high literature. Think for instance about Scott's *Ivanhoe.*[17]

The heroic scenario is not a genre, but a structure that can be found, directly or indirectly, in all literary genres, even love stories. The structure of love stories often comprises the overcoming of obstacles and of adversaries who delay the happy end, the reunion of the lovers. One of the earliest examples of the genre, *Le Chevalier de la Charrette* (c. 1180), directly illustrates this structure.[18]

Literature is a play with the structure, a more or less complex play.

7. A Unique Goal, from Childhood On

To be the Hero of History. It is the ultimate goal that each one pursues from childhood to adulthood.

There is a childish heroic scenario just like there is an adult one. The adult scenario is merely a transformed version of the childish one. No one ever renounces to be the Hero of History, neither the child nor the adult. The adult understanding of the world is different. It evolved. But it is still in continuity with the child's.

The childish heroic scenario is on a scale with the child's knowledge of the world. Children see their role as preserving the family circle: the parents, caretakers, brothers and sisters who are originally the only objects of affection. They want to keep the loved ones forever united and happy.

Adults have long learned that the family circle cannot be defended and preserved forever, but they accept that a larger group, the nation, can. Yet, the adult continues to be inspired by the child's goal, and the national history is but an extended version of the childish heroic scenario.

The transformation of the childish vision of history into a national history is revealed by associations of ideas that would not otherwise be explainable. The national history evokes many elements belonging to the early heroic scenario nurtured in childhood. For instance, nation and family are constantly associated in the national history.

The "nation" literally means the group where a people are born, like a family. The connection with the idea of the family is actually so strong that the nation may also be called the "fatherland" or the "motherland" or even the "mother country." It can be represented as a mother, a woman named Marianne in France, Britannia in Britain, or Germania in Germany. Moreover, the national history starts like a family story: the nation often has a founding "father" such as Romulus in Ancient Rome, or Atatürk, "the Father of the Turks" Mustafa Kemal, first president of the Turkish Republic.

Like the history of the family, the national history is conceived as a chapter of a bigger narrative. The nation is imagined to belong to a family of nations, like the family circle revealed itself to be a part of an extended family. The national language, the medium through which the national spirit is passed from one generation to the next, is, like the nation, said to be related to a family. Languages are supposed to have cousins and common ancestors, like people, and nations. The history of a linguistic family can be represented as a family tree with branches. It may include older languages and even "dead" ones.

Nation and family are thus two closely connected ideas. It is the result of the transformation of the early childish vision of history into the national history familiar to adults.

The first heroic scenario is nurtured in the earliest childhood, when the parents or caretakers are the child's only companions, the ones helping the child through the first pains, tantrums, explorations and joys. From the earliest days, the child experiences extreme dependency on these closest relations. Separation from them is felt with the greatest pain, and every possible effort is made to bring the pain to an end. At that stage, the child dreams of protecting the family circle forever.

In consequence, children are extremely interested in growing up and in imitating the grown-ups: they want to be able to stay with them and to accompany them in all their activities. They blame themselves when they are separated from their parents or when parents fight.

This early heroic scenario unravels as the child gains a more specific knowledge of social rules and discovers that the family circle depends on a larger social order. Before that stage, the child's desire to be united with the parents remained generally undiscussed. Love for the parents was simply praised. However, knowledge of social rules allows the child to be more specific about the possible ways to stay forever with the parents. If, for instance, having learned of marriage, a boy starts considering marrying his mother, he is bound to face rebuttals, not only directly from his parents, but also from observations of other people, none of whom married their own parents. Thus, the discovery of a larger society is fatal for the early heroic scenario.

The child does not, however, easily accept the result and seeks by all means to ignore it. The simplest way to imagine being one day capable of preserving forever the unity of the family, in spite of the parents, is to imagine that the parents have lied about being the true parents. It is the single simplest change that allows the continuation of the nurturing of the original heroic scenario. The child can also dream that the real parents are a very powerful and rich couple. They would certainly have the means to curb social rules to their advantage and make sure the family remains united forever. Depending on the child's knowledge and on the society's culture, they may be seen as billionaires or a king and queen. Lastly the child is bound to imagine that they must not know of their heir's survival or they would have searched and found them. Kidnap and adoption by the official parents is a frequent solution.[1] Feelings for the official parents tend to be ambivalent; their inadequate status is resented while a final reconciliation is very much desired nonetheless.

Nobody's Boy by Hector Malot [2] is a fictional story inspired by this early stage of the "family romance." Rémi, a boy aged eight, discovers brutally that he is not the son of Mother Barberin who raised him. The man whom he thought was his father sells him to a street musician, Vitalis. However, the old man proves a worthy caretaker and educator. After many adventures, during which Vitalis dies, Rémi discovers the secret of his origins and the name of his real mother: Mrs. Milligan, an aristocratic English woman. Rémi happens to know her. He actually met her in southern France and entertained her handicapped boy. Rémi learns that he was kidnapped as a baby. He gathers evidence and finds Mrs. Milligan again, who recognizes him as her lost son. Rémi and the friends he made during his ordeal, as well as Mother Barberin, are eventually all sheltered by Mrs. Milligan. They live happily together ever after.

Family romance facilitates the child's interest in social life outside the family circle. To find the lost parents, the child must learn about the vast world and enlist new companions. These new companions become, in turn, people to keep close. Family romance fantasies evolve. The circle of companions gets larger.

This more advanced stage of the family romance inspired, for example, Michael Crichton's *Timeline*. [3] Professor Johnson, an archeologist, time-travels to the fourteenth century. There, a cruel warlord makes him prisoner. His students, joined by his son, follow him in the past, defeat the warlord, and bring the professor back. Contrary to the early family romance, the people to be found and saved in this scenario are not simply parents in substitution. The professor is not simply a substitute of the father. He is both professor and father. A more complex world has emerged in the family romance. To save his father, one character has to trust his father's students, learn from them, and enlist them in the rescuing mission. These new companions become, in turn, people to love and save.

Increasingly complex fantasies illustrate how the family romance gets incrementally extended into an international history and how being unable to preserve forever the family circle becomes acceptable. New companions are recognized, and these new relations capture a part of the affection that used to be the monopoly of the parents and caretakers. It becomes possible to consider saving and preserving forever that more complex, evolving, network of relations, especially once they are understood as a much extended sort of family, a nation.

The family romance leaves traces in the national and international histories that are elaborated from it. They often retain episodes that are directly inspired by family romance fantasies. These episodes are notably present in the legendary and extraordinary lives of founders of nations. Many examples were gathered by Otto Rank. They contain stories of children whose lives are threatened at a very early age, often after having been abandoned by their real high-status parents. They are then discovered by humble people who take care of them. Their extraordinary deeds in adolescence reveal their superior nature and signal the start of their social rise. They are often reunited with their real parents in the end. Rank discovered this common structure by analyzing no less than fifty-six legends, including the lives of: Sargon, Etana, Moses, Osiris, Ahi, Thoth, Mani-Tiki-Tiki, Abraham, Isaac, Joseph, Karna, Ion,

Oedipus, Judah, Gregory, Darab, Paris, Zal, Telephus, Perseus, Dionysus, Apollo, Ainus, Adonis, Erichthonius, Gilgamesh, Cyrus, Kai Khosrau, David, Brutus, Tell, Vaïnämöinen, Hamlet, Kullervo, Kalevi Poëg, Feridun, Trakhan, Romulus, Amphion and Zethus, Heracles, Krishna, Jesus, Zoroaster, Buddha, Mithra, Siegfried, Wolfdietrich, Horn, Wieland, Tristan, Lohengrin, Tyro and Scéaf. Rank also mentions legends from Singapore, Maui, Tonga, and Betsinisaraka.[4]

Sigmund Freud interpreted the story of Moses as a partial exception to Rank's structure because Moses was the son of humble slaves instead of being born in a royal or wealthy family. He was adopted by the daughter of Pharaoh instead of being raised by poor shepherds.[5] The rest of the legend is fairly typical: Moses discovered his true origins as a young man, and the discovery changed his life forever. He revolted against the slavery imposed by the Egyptians on the Hebrews and left Egypt to live in the desert. There, he met God who made him His agent to liberate the Hebrews and lead them in the Promised Land.

Freud supposed that the partial inversion of the legend came from a late revision: Moses was originally an Egyptian character who became a Jewish national hero. Freud quoted Josephus who reported a version of the legend according to which Moses was the son or the grandson of Pharaoh.[6] Freud's interpretation of Egyptian origins is plausible; however, the legend is no exception. By serving God and His chosen people, Moses elevated himself above his former condition as an Egyptian prince, and he vanquished Pharaoh. Having been adopted by Egyptians revealed itself a degrading condition in spite of the apparent power and wealth of Pharaoh. God's power was greater. Thus, the story of Moses is just as typical of the influence of the family romance as the other legends collected by Rank. It only differs from them by the absence of final reconciliation with the adopting family.

The national community is imagined to be a very large, much extended family, so that the family circle is a part of a larger family. To defend the nation is to preserve some continuity within the family as well. This is illustrated by an Irish language activist, Sarah Ó Sullivan, who explained to me why she chose to promote Gaelic schooling: "I did not want to be the one who would break the chain":

> Irish Gaelic was recently spoken in our families. My grandmother and her mother were the first generations to speak English. They did not turn away from Gaelic because of English garrisons, or famine, or poverty. But as more and more of their friends died or emigrated, they found themselves utterly alone and deprived. They felt they had no choice anymore.

> My Mother was born in 1909. She first learned Gaelic at school, not at home. Later she spent summers in the Gaelic community and joined the Gaelic League. She was a famous Gaelic singer. As a child, I was quite aware of the importance of Gaelic.

> When I was ten, my mother and I went to a meeting held by Eamon de Valera, the first President of the Irish Free State. He stood on the back of a truck and spoke Gaelic for a while. I thought he did it for me.

> At school teachers passed on to us their love for the language. One was a fluent Gaelic speaker, the other an admirer of Patrick Pearse, the Irish Independence Hero. I later joined the Gaelic League in spite of the admonitions of my priest. In the League, I made friends. We spoke Gaelic. And I met my husband....[7]

Sarah Ó Sullivan's account is a testimony of how defending the national heritage can finally be perceived to be a way of maintaining elements of unity and continuity within the family. The acceptance of a national history allows the adult to fulfill much of the original heroic scenario. Being the defender of the nation and of the family circle appears one and the same thing.

To defend one's family effectively, one needs to find allies and defend a whole nation. The nation appears to be the only really defendable circle. This idea inspired stories such as the movie *The Patriot.* [8] A wealthy man refuses to join the American insurgents in 1776. However, when the British kill one of his sons and are preparing to execute a second, he feels compelled to join the insurgents and attack the British patrol that took his son prisoner. His military skills soon make him a leader of the insurgents.

Parents and caretakers are perceived as companions again, people who show the way and inspire the right actions. Although there might have been some divergences with them at some point, it all makes sense in the end. Inversely, failure to find a place among companions in a national kinship often re-ignites family romance fantasies, bringing back ill-feelings towards parents. For instance, a perception of military, marital or professional failure can trigger such a regression. These adult family fantasies are often referred to as family secret fantasies. Childish desires of powerful parents endure but have become more subtle. Adults who entertain a feeling of failure tend to imagine that they are disadvantaged by a sin or a mistake committed by their ancestors and kept secret from them by their parents. Discovering it, repairing it, or being absolved from it is imagined to be a necessary step to succeed in personal endeavors. By association, the discovery of the family secret is often imagined to enable triumph over the Enemy.

Such fantasies inspired, for instance, the final book in the *Harry Potter* series, *The Deathly Hallows.*[9] Harry Potter has become an adult. But he feels that he will not be able to defeat the evil Lord Voldemort because his former headmaster, Albus Dumbledore, hid many dark secrets. He did not reveal them to Harry before he died. Harry is an orphan and calls his former school, Hogwarts, home. The headmaster's family secrets are akin to a family secret. Only after Harry's friends, Ron and Hermione, helped him uncover the whole truth about his own origins and Dumbledore's past, can Harry, reconciled with his former headmaster, challenge Voldemort and defeat him at last.

Another famous example is the *Star Wars* trilogy. The first movie is inspired by a rather early type of family romance, but the last two draw distinctively upon the themes of the family secret, as if the audience was expected to mature a little. In the first movie, *A New Hope,*[10] the young Luke Skywalker is raised by his foster parents, modest farmers on the desert planet Tatooine, a backwater of the Galactic Empire. An old hermit, Obi-Wan Kenobi, reveals to Luke that his real father was a Jedi knight whose special powers Luke inherited. He also tells Luke that his father was killed by the Emperor's deputy, Darth Vader. When his foster parents are brutally murdered by imperial squadrons, Luke decides to join the Rebel Alliance and fight the evil Empire. With his new friends, Luke brings decisive help to the beleaguered Alliance and destroys the Empire's ultimate weapon, the Death Star. In the second episode, *The Empire Strikes Back,*[11] Luke meets Vader at last, but Vader reveals that he really is Luke's father. The revelation of the secret shatters Luke, who resents intensely the lies of Obi-Wan Kenobi. In the third episode, *The Return of the Jedi,*[12] Luke realizes he does not want to fight his father and tries to liberate him from the Emperor's influence. In the end, when all seems lost, Vader saves his son by killing the Emperor and so redeems himself before succumbing to his wounds. The family secret contained the key to victory.

The family secret fantasy is the last stage in the family romance fantasies. It illustrates the long and often cumbersome transition from the childish heroic scenario to the national history that is the frame of adult life.

Adults continue to be secretly inspired by childish reminiscences. These intimate notions, that are never shared with others, make them feel that they have a deeper, more intimate connection with the danger that other people seem to have. This sense of uniqueness reinforces the notion of being the Chosen One, called to action by a special destiny.

*

Early in the twentieth century, the striking resemblances between the legendary lives of many national heroes suggested some universal cause. Otto Rank and Sigmund Freud admitted that these resemblances could have been due to imitations. Influences between people, even extremely remote in space and time, can never completely be ruled out, but then, they argued, even imitations had to be explained by a convergent taste, which could only be ascribed to a common fundamental predisposition of the mind.[13] This was a breakthrough in the discovery of a universal structure of the mind.

Freud proposed an explanation centered on what he called the repression of the Oedipus Complex. He thought that the legends were attractive because they would express otherwise repressed feelings. According to Freud, the young boy would desire to possess exclusively his mother and would be jealous of his father whom he would want to eliminate and replace. The boy would also admire his father and would want to imitate him, which would reinforce his jealousy. Freud supposed that these feelings would later be repressed in the unconscious part of the mind, which would explain why they could reappear only in adults suffering breakdowns or in artistic works, when repression is less strong. In order to explain the repression, Freud proposed that the child also develops what he termed a "castration complex." The child would fear for himself. He would be afraid that his father would punish him for his feelings.[14]

According to Freud, the fantasies related to the family romance would result from the repression of the Oedipus Complex. Indeed, like earlier fantasies, they appear to be generally abandoned before adulthood.[15] Freud also proposed that the repression of the Oedipus Complex would endure into adulthood because the original fear of the wrath of the father would be prolonged by the fear of other powerful people: the chief, the captain or the king. This is why they are all considered by Freud to be figures of the father. According to him, the repression of the Oedipus Complex would thus be the key tendency that structures social life. It would also make legends appealing and universally resembling. The legends would be rare outlets through which repressed desires could be expressed and satisfaction could be found.

But the Freudian theory is not supported by the facts. If it were, all legends would be built on a different scenario than the one which is universally observed. First, the hero would be threatened by his father. Second, he would kill his father. Third, he would marry his mother. No legend matches, even remotely, this scenario. Freud might have been aware of this as he never claimed that marriage to the mother is a common pattern of a legend. However, he maintained that all the legends gathered by Rank share one common pattern: the hero's father would have tried to kill his son, and the hero would have had to fight against his father in order to survive. "A hero is a man who stands up manfully against his father and in the end victoriously overcomes him."[16]

The evidence invoked by Freud contradicts his theory: the legendary heroes never attack their fathers. On the contrary, they are quite eager to defend them against aggression and tyranny or to avenge them. The same can be said regarding other relatives. Most legends reflect strong filial or familial love. Bonds are sometimes tested, but they prove strong.

For example, the young Romulus and Remus ignore their real family. They fight against their grandfather's servants, but once they discover their true origins, they instantly join their grandfather and fight to reinstall him on the throne of Alba. In another exemplary story, Joseph is sold as a slave by his jealous brothers, yet he pardons them and rescues them in the end along with their beloved father.

Even the legend singled out by Freud as the most typical of the supposedly repressed feelings hardly fits this explanation. The life of Oedipus by Sophocles (c. 429 BCE) is a tragedy, not an epic drama.[17]

When Oedipus was born, an oracle predicted that he would kill his father. Terrified, his father, the king, ordered his son to be executed, but the soldier in charge of that mission abandoned the baby in the wild where he was miraculously found by a poor shepherd who raised him. The young adult Oedipus, unaware of his royal origins, traveled and sought distinction abroad. On the road, he met an arrogant lord, fought him, and killed him. He later freed the city of Thebes from a rapacious monster, the Sphinx; was elected King; married the recently widowed queen; and had children with her. When a plague fell on the city, an oracle revealed that Oedipus was the son of the late king he had killed and of the queen he had married. Desperate, Oedipus blinded himself and left Thebes, never to come back.

If the legend of Oedipus were an opportunity to express a repressed lust for the mother or a repressed hostility towards the father, the reader would feel aroused. It is even possible to imagine that in the end, in order to satisfy the reader's repressed desires, Oedipus would find some way to remain king and husband to his mother. The killing of his father would be celebrated. Our feelings, however, are dominated by pity for Oedipus and anger at the undeserved destiny imposed on him by the gods. At no point can the reader feel elation. The Oedipus Complex" theory neither fits the legend nor the reader's reaction to it. Oedipus's legendary life was a tragedy. For all his wits, courage and honesty, Oedipus had no control over the events; he was a mere puppet for the gods. They punished him harshly for crimes he did not even know he had committed. The gods appear unjust because they recognized a father in a man who had not recognized his own son, who was not a father according to the laws and the gods themselves. There seemed to be no mitigating circumstances in the victory over the Sphinx either.

Freud's theory does not explain Hamlet any better either. Yet Hamlet was the second case that he singled out as typically inspired by the Oedipus Complex.[18] Freud asserted that in Shakespeare's play, Hamlet procrastinates and does not dare to avenge his father's death.[19] Freud explained that Hamlet's inaction was motivated by an unconscious admiration for the murderer, his uncle and his father's brother, who married the widow, Hamlet's mother, to become King of Denmark in place of his victim.

If Freud's explanation were correct, Hamlet would never have happily killed the murderer in the end, and he would not have been so deeply depressed in the beginning. In fact, Freud neglects to take into account one key element introduced by Shakespeare: no one knows that Hamlet's uncle is the assassin. Hamlet himself does not dare believe it, and he has every reason to do so as he learned it from a ghost who claimed to be the soul of his dead father. Hamlet wants further evidence and, in the absence of it, becomes depressed by uncertainty and inaction. He loses self-esteem and faith in loved ones. He yearns, however, to avenge his father, and he seizes, shortly before his own death, the first opportunity available when his uncle at last reveals his perfidy.

Finally, it is surprising that neither Rank nor Freud considered the legend that, at first glance, seems to fit best the Oedipus Complex theory: the legend of Zeus. The father of Zeus, Chronos, had made a habit of eating his children. The mother of Zeus saved her son by hiding him from his father. When Zeus became an adult, he vanquished Chronos and emasculated him, liberating his brothers and sisters, still contained in Chronos. Yet, even in that particularly extreme scenario, there is an element of filial reconciliation in the end, for Zeus actually reunites Chronos with his children.

In these many legends, the usual adversary is not the father; instead, he is a tyrant who oppresses the hero and his family. None of the legends truly fits the Oedipus Complex hypothesis. If this hypothesis was correct, the legends that people entertain would be quite different, and the ones passed on would not be attractive at all. Rank eventually conceded that the father is not the adversary of the hero and that the desire to protect and save him dominates the legends.[20]

8. A Unique, Intimate Enemy

Deep inside, unaware, each one entertains the notion of an intimate Enemy, a hidden being, uniquely malevolent and dangerous, who wants to upset the world order and dominate all things.

The mere evocation of a danger brings about images of a person, or at least of a body, often a threatening one. This happens even in circumstances where these ideas could seem quite incongruous. This can only be explained by the superior attractiveness of the idea of the Enemy.

The evocation of a danger generates associations with simultaneous ideas that could seem quite incompatible otherwise. The mind associates all types of dangers in imagining the Enemy. He is conceived as the unique source of all dangers.

The evocation of a danger thus creates a sense of an intimate experience. It evokes ideas that are unlikely to have been shared or discussed but are likely to be purely personal, such as childish fantasies. It seems that other people are not equally aware of the presence of the Enemy. Being hidden thus seems part of his plans. It seems to reinforce the danger.

Fiction and historical narratives equally reflect the attractiveness of the idea of the Enemy. Let us consider three examples: a fiction, a fundraising campaign and cartoons published by an activist magazine.

Firstly, in the movie *The Perfect Storm*,[1] a poor fisher decides to undertake one last fishing trip to make up for a series of poor catches. He ventures much farther than usual. The weather is calm, but appearances are deceiving; the most extraordinary storm is brewing. At last, a friend manages to make radio contact with the fisher and warns him that he is "heading towards the jaw of a monster." Unfortunately, it is too late to rescue him.

The Perfect Storm is typical of ideas associated with the Enemy. The story is based on a danger that is not embodied, a storm, but that attracts this idea nonetheless, as is revealed by the evocation of "the jaw of a monster." This image typically evokes childish fantasies and nightmares populated with animal monsters. It is certainly not a convention between fishers to label storms that way. The danger comes stealthily, although the public knows of course, in advance, what to expect. All the typical notions associated with the Enemy are present.

Secondly, the Pasteur Institute posted an advertisement for a fundraising campaign on the 30th anniversary of the discovery of AIDS. The advertisement shows a bullet that tears apart an AIDS virus. On one side, the virus has a typical shape, reminiscent of a naval mine: spherical with antennas protruding in all directions. On the other side, the bullet evokes a human or animal body, not a virus. It would be absurd otherwise; a virus is far too small to be destroyed by a bullet. This image was designed to emphasize that in spite of its lack of apparent danger due to its small size, the corpuscle was actually a stealthy killer and had to be treated as such.

Implicitly, the danger and the determination to kill the virus were perceived to be better evoked by the suggestion of a very classic, even simplistic way to kill: with a revolver, something that a child could imagine, that a single person could do. This was perceived to be a more effective image than that of armies of researchers in laboratories. To show a single virus was perceived more effective than to show billions of them replicating. In short, the Pasteur Institute believed it more attractive to suggest a unique, embodied and intimate threat.

Already in 1900, the Institute's management saw microbes as too elusive adversaries to be presented as they were under the microscope. A funding campaign associated microbes and monsters of all kinds (Figure 5).

Pasteur's new methods of inoculation were deliberately portrayed as "wars" on microbes. In France, they were linked to revenge against Prussian Germany. Microbes were often labeled "Prussian" in the French press, and Prussia was often compared to an infection as if all these dangers, microbiotic and international, were linked. As if they were all simply one unique danger. Latour observed that this mode of designation of the microscopic adversaries indeed helped make new treatments popular and successful.[2]

Figure 5. Microbes as monsters in a 1900 advertising campaign by Anios / Pasteur Institute.[3]

The logo of the René Schickele Circle drawn by Tomi Ungerer in 1992 is our third example. It represented a giant that squeezed a little man's foot under his huge shoe. The giant was at least ten times bigger than his victim. He was so tall that only his huge leg appeared on the drawing. The little man shouted to the giant: "My foot [in French]... is a foot! [in Alsatian]." The French language has the same expression as does the English: treading on the little man's toes, the giant shows him his contempt and usurps his rights. However, the little man resists by claiming his right to physical integrity and to speak

104

both French and Alsatian. The Circle seeks to defend Alsace against "Frenchization."

Ungerer's giant is a typical image of the Enemy. First, he embodies physical threat and oppression. Second, the idea is an intimate notion, one that evokes strongly childish memories. Giants are typically the product of a child's imagination. They are also quite popular in fairy tales, such as *Little Poucet* (*Hop o' My Thumb*) by Charles Perrault (*Figure 6*).[4] Third, the giant's face remains characteristically hidden. Four, he embodies a unique threat; his sheer size alone suggests it.

This interpretation is confirmed by another drawing in which the same giant's foot is placed on a map of France at the location of Paris, while the little man does not protest only in French and Alsatian, but also in Basque, Breton, Occitan, etc., as if all the people speaking these languages faced the same threat, a unique danger coming from Paris. At the time of its publication, members of the Schickele Circle indeed accused "Paris" and "the Ministries" of engineering the demise of the Alsatian language and all its sister languages in France.

A convergent drawing was made by another defender of the Alsatian language, Robert Piela.[5] The aggressor, a tailor, also from Paris, wanted to cut the tongue of an Alsatian-speaking child. The attack is typical of a child's imagination; it evokes nursery rhymes such as:

Tell Tale Tit
Your tongue shall be slit
And all the little dicky-birds will have a little bit.

Figure 6. The giant as a childish nightmare (Gustave Doré's 1867 illustration for Hop o' My Thumb).

In both cases, the wrongdoer came from a single place: Paris. The unique origin of all evils is a characteristic notion associated with the Enemy. To mention the Enemy's dwelling place is a direct way to evoke him as he is supposed to be hidden there. Activists defending the Alsatian language designated "Paris" as the source of evil, while defenders of the Welsh language speak of "London" and "Westminster" to designate the origins of the woes that they denounce. However, they all regard the most public figures, elected officials or members of the reigning family, as rather benign people.[6] Likewise, the opponents of the communist block during the Cold War were convinced that "Moscow" was plotting against the Free World; however, they were willing to meet with Soviet leaders and negotiate with them. In all these cases, the Enemy was always suspected to remain hidden in his lair.

In all these examples, the Enemy is imagined as a unique will from which all evils derive. He is hidden. Only an intimate knowledge of his actions helps to detect and reveal the danger.

The notion of an intimate connection with the Enemy is very often conveyed by images reminiscent of childish fantasies. These images illustrate and reinforce the idea that one is facing the same malevolent will since childhood. For example, most Alsatian activists I interviewed mentioned that they had personally been victims of the schooling system as children. They mentioned that they had been punished for speaking Alsatian at school, forced to carry a shameful "symbol." The Welsh activists I met also spontaneously produced personal anecdotes concerning the use of a more brutal technique used to eradicate Welsh from Welsh schools: a stick labeled the "Welsh Not".[7]

The idea that one has been facing a single threat since childhood also inspires fiction. For example, in *LA Confidential,*[8] an adult finally meets the Enemy he dreamed of as a child.

At the beginning of the movie, three young Los Angeles police officers, Bud White, Jack Vincennes and Ed Exley evolve in a Los Angeles Police Department that has little to do with the ideal LAPD of televised fictions "inspired by real events." Far from always bringing justice or defending morality, each officer incarnates a particularly un-heroic aspect of the real LAPD. White is thuggish and racist, Vincennes is obsessively mundane, and Exley is an individualist and careerist. Each one despises the others. Exley resents the brutality of White, who in return, cannot bear Exley's cunning in advancing his own career at the expense of both his colleagues. Both see Vincennes as a degenerated cop who selects investigations that are most likely to make him a front-page hero no matter what compromises with the truth this entails.

Each finds in his past dubious justifications for his behavior: Exley is the son of a heroic father, also a detective, who died in service when Exley was a young boy, to whom he is constantly compared, at his disadvantage; White is obsessed with bringing justice to wife beaters because he witnessed his father kill his mother. Only Captain Dudley Smith seems capable of bringing some restraint to such highly dysfunctional personalities and making them occasionally work together.

A crime at the Nite Owl café, where a colleague is killed, draws their attention. Although the case has been rapidly closed by the death of the three main suspects, White, Vincennes and Exley have each a reason to be dissatisfied. Separately, they come to realize that the murders are linked to a large quantity of heroin smuggled from the ancient Mafioso boss, Mickey Cohen. Someone is trying to replace Cohen and control the drug traffic in LA. A sense of danger looming brings Vincennes and Exley closer, and Exley confesses an intimate fantasy. Because his father was murdered and the case was never solved, Exley imagined when he was a child that his father's murderer was a very bad guy named "Rollo Tomasi." Rollo Tomasi is the guy who "got away with it," was never suspected, and was never discovered. One night, Vincennes pays a private visit to the Captain Dudley Smith to get some advice on the affair. Smith suddenly kills Vincennes, revealing himself to be the new mafia boss. Just before he dies, Vincennes whispers: "Rollo Tomasi." His body is found in a park the next morning. No connection with Smith is made.

Intrigued by the name "Rollo Tomasi," Smith casually drops it in a conversation with Exley, not knowing that it was Exley's secret fantasy and that Vincennes was the only one to share it. Exley now knows that Smith killed Vincennes. Suddenly "Rollo Tomasi" seems to materialize in front of him. Exley says nothing but Smith senses the surge in tension in him and knows he must eliminate him. He turns White against Exley by showing him pictures of Exley naked with Lynn, White's girlfriend. The maneuver almost serves its purpose, but White ultimately rallies to Exley in order to save Lynn. Together they encounter their common adversary and kill him.

Fiction and historical accounts equally contain references to an intimate Enemy, a hidden being, uniquely malevolent and dangerous, who wants to upset the world order and dominate all things. In fiction, only the hero seems to have a special, intimate knowledge of the Enemy's presence. This knowledge transpires in historical accounts too. The authors of historical accounts share with the fictional hero an intimate knowledge of the Enemy.

III

Making History

Each of us is irresistibly attracted, without ever being aware of it, by the vision of a heroic destiny which will confront them to an all-powerful Enemy.

Most people, however, live in peace time, when there is no clear immediate threat. Not even the remotest rumors about the Enemy may be heard. When the Enemy is thus strangely absent from everyday life, people are more inclined to feel boredom, meaninglessness. They react against these inadequate circumstances by engaging in day-dreaming or by consuming fiction, since fiction is then more attractive than reality.

But that does not suffice. They have a nagging notion that reality is not quite as peaceful and unthreatening as it seems. They may ascribe it to imagination, but it keeps returning. Indeed, the absence of the Enemy from everyday life is not at all a problem for the mind. Its perceived absence does not make him any less real to the mind that produces the idea. And since the Enemy is primarily thought of as a will, the mind easily makes sense of the situation by imagining that the Enemy wants to hide and manipulate his victims. The secret of his existence must be his most powerful weapon.

People thus feel in themselves a special awareness that they cannot detect in others. But they dare not move on their own. They imagine that the history that has been told to them is purposefully incomplete and misleading. They fear they might be manipulated themselves. They hover between self-doubt and self-blame for not knowing how to recognize good from evil.

The only way to be delivered from doubt is to meet companions, people willing to share their most intimate thoughts, to have no secrets. And the only way to make sure they have no secret is to evoke with them intimate fears and to find confirmation in their reactions that one is not completely foolish. Indeed, evoking the Enemy's plans certainly cannot be his design for he is imagined to remain voluntarily hidden.

With companions one feels confident, capable of uncovering conspiracies and revealing deception. What is confirmed by companions is regarded as true. In fact, they are the only source of truth. Everything else is doubtful. Thus as everyone wants to know the truth, everyone spontaneously seeks companions and adjusts to their worldview *(9 – Revealed Truths)*.

The more fellow fighters recognize each other, the less they doubt themselves. Their mobilization accelerates *(10–Telling Friends from Foes)*.

The mobilization is bipolar. The more people find companions and the more they are mobilized against people they see as their adversaries. Each one increasingly recognizes the reality they aspire to, where there are only two camps: adversaries and companions. All adversaries are considered to belong to a single camp, whatever their differences. Indeed, they must all ultimately serve the Enemy, the unique source of all evils. In turn, all the adversaries of the adversaries are imagined to belong to a single camp, because they all ultimately fight the Enemy. They are all imagined to be friends and allies. Interactions increasingly reinforce two sides. Two hostile coalitions build up: as the bipolar mobilization accelerates, it attracts ever larger numbers.

The Enemy hides. Provocations are necessary to make him react and reveal his evil nature. The more adversaries react, the more the activists find their provocations vindicated by the new turn of events. They also find renewed inspiration in every reaction they elicit. Thus, from provocation to reaction, both sides create new circumstances which justify their actions and attract more and more people to their cause. As the general bipolarization accelerates, it makes all converge on a new vision of History *(11-* Converging Visions of History*)*

The general bipolarization peaks when both sides, sufficiently converged, are in accordance not only about the general direction of history, but also about the ways and means that must decide the outcome of the conflict. As a result, when the conflict reaches its climax, in spite of an extreme mutual hostility, both sides can agree on which side won and which side lost. Victory and defeat are followed by a general demobilization. The Enemy seems gone. The general bipolarization goes through cycles. It accelerates, peaks and then decelerates. But the end of a cycle is not the End of History. It is immediately followed by the beginning of another cycle of bipolar alliances and conflicts.

Successive cycles lead to increasingly large coalitions facing each other. Former adversaries have come to share a common vision of history. They can become allies against common adversaries. Convergence over many successive cycles of alliances and conflicts make more and more people share a common international history. An international society emerges. It brings together all the people who recognize each other as worthy allies and adversaries *(12 –The International Bipolarization)*.

All personal actions, ambitions and rivalries must converge and align with the general bipolarization *(13–From Personal*

Rivalries to World War). The ubiquity of conflict dynamics is hard to accept though. Each one would spontaneously prefer people to be generally reasonable and peaceful. But precisely, they also resent other people not behaving so. These notions also foster bipolarization (*14–Beyond Reason and Above All Laws*).

9. Revealed Truths

Each one is driven to imagine they are the Hero. But the Enemy one intimately feels must exist is nowhere to be seen. He must hide, the better to manipulate his victims. It is impossible to know where evil is and to distinguish evil from good. Self-doubt creeps in. It is impossible to act. Paralysis in the face of the Enemy must be his doing. One is driven to blame oneself. Self-doubt and self-blame alternate endlessly, reinforcing each other in a vicious loop. The only thing that is finally certain is that one is increasingly isolated, unable to reach out. Isolation is certainly the ultimate evil.

At that point, anyone who is not blaming you but merely treating you as a peer is lifting you up, relieving self-doubt and self-hatred, acting as a companion. The more companions are capable of listening to your fears, the more they open a door onto a world where good can be distinguished from evil. There is some certainty after all. Companions are the ultimate good.

This drive to socialize has taken place since the origins of the life of the mind, even before the mind was capable of elaborating any scenario that could be shared.

The mind is constantly driven to anticipate and imagine disruptions. In its own experience it is therefore itself a chief source of disruptions. Furthermore, it is driven to imagine, behind each actual disruption, a will similar to its own. People are attracted above all by disruptions and therefore by other people, which they imagine as their fellow beings, their peers, their equals. They project their own self onto them. They imagine their wills and their faces even where there is none.

They are ambivalent about these peers like they are about themselves. They intimately know they are capable of doing evil as well as good. But people want to distinguish good from evil, to know one from the other. They therefore want to know better who people really are. It is all about knowing how to recognize evil from good, in others like in oneself.

Learning to distinguish oneself from other causes, from other people, and learning to distinguish good from evil, is one indistinguishable journey that starts with the first movement of the mind and lasts all life long. The key is always the same. One must find peers with whom to learn to distinguish good from evil. The more one has companions, the more one feels one can distinguish oneself, and be the Hero.

People spontaneously seek companions. This can be observed in toddlers like in adults. It belongs to the spontaneous and universal tendencies of the mind. This tendency has crucial consequences.

Without companions, people simply turn against themselves. They do this without even thinking about it. The mind is made to react to the information that it perceives. Isolated from other people, companions or adversaries, the mind spontaneously detects willful perturbations in the only source where it can find them, its own physical activities. It reacts against them and turns to actively disrupting them. The body underperforms. Isolated babies are particularly at risk. They have not yet learned what is proper to themselves and to others. It is for them a most deadly situation, especially if prolonged. Young children also suffer disproportionately when isolated.

This was first observed and recorded in thirteenth-century southern Italy. Emperor Frederick II conducted an experiment to determine the natural speech of humans. He gathered dozens of newborns and instructed their foster-mothers and nurses to suckle, bathe and wash them, but under no circumstances to play with them or speak. He hoped to record the language the children would spontaneously use without having ever heard any other before. His main expectations were Latin, Hebrew or Greek. But none of these languages was spoken by any of the infants. All died prematurely without having spoken a recognizable word.[1]

To a lesser degree, a comparable situation was observed by the psychoanalyst René Spitz with orphaned children placed in institutions. The institutions focused on the threat of germs. The children were well fed, kept warm and clean, but had limited contact with playmates and caretakers to limit microbiotic transmission. Indeed, orphans who got contaminated were particularly in danger. The average death rate from measles reached, for example, 40 percent compared with 5 percent in ordinary children. Spitz proposed that isolation and lack of interaction actually increased fatality.[2]

This hypothesis was confirmed as young animals experiencing prolonged isolation from their mothers were observed to produce sharp drops in vitality indicators, such as hormonal levels and temperature, while body rhythms, such as heart rate and sleep, were increasing irregular.[3]

If the mind was simply adjusting through empathy with other people, psychic activities would not necessarily be affected by the absence of the companion. The state of mind installed in presence of the companions might well continue even in their absence. Only the presence of a person could affect it, not their absence. In fact, in the absence of the loved ones the mind actively disrupts the body's activities, shutting them down or producing wild fluctuations. This reaction differentiates the mind's working from simple empathy. It also shows that there is no such thing as a survival instinct.

Babies, like children and adults, need someone to deliver them from their terrors, to help them calm down. Companions are necessary to distinguish good from evil and truth from lies. The truth is therefore what companions say it is. The truth is always revealed. People always believe that companions do the right thing. They are driven to the worldview of their companions. As a consequence, people anticipate their companions' every feeling, even their most intimate ones. And they tend to adjust to them. They tend to synchronize with them.

This happened for example in the Spanish village of San Pedro Manrique when, every June 23rd, its inhabitants celebrated the summer solstice with religious processions. At midnight, they organized a special ritual. People "walked on fire." They crossed a 23-foot-long carpet of red-hot oak embers barefooted and carrying another person on their back. This ceremony took place in a special amphitheater built for three-thousand spectators, much in excess of the five-hundred villagers. Each year the ritual attracts many tourists. Ivana Konvalinka and her team of researchers monitored the heart rate of twelve fire-walkers, nine spectators related to fire-walkers and seventeen tourists. The spectators simply watched, without sharing activity or rhythm with the fire walkers. The heart rates of relatives and friends of the fire-walkers rose and decreased in synchrony with those of the fire-walkers, although not with the same amplitude.[4]

This observation showed that deep synchronization could not merely be the result of moving together to the rhythm, like when singing, dancing or marching together. Vickhoff and fellow researchers had explained the synchronization of pulses in choir singers by synchronized breathing.[5] But something deeper operates. And it also explains, in the case described by Vickhoff, why the singers meet and find pleasure in singing. Their synchronization can only be the observable result of their desire for fellowship.

Synchronization extends beyond emotions and body rhythms to cognition and narratives. Since companions are necessary to distinguish good from evil and truth from lies, the truth is what companions say it is. The truth is always revealed.

This spontaneous understanding of the world has been observed even in babies. An experiment was designed to observe babies using their companions' – in that case, their mother's – knowledge to decide which direction to take. They simply learned from observing their mother's state of mind, reading their faces.

The experiment used a plexiglass table. The surface was partly opaque and partly transparent. Babies were placed on the opaque part and allowed to move freely. Their mothers remained close by but did not help physically. The babies typically moved until they reached the place where the surface became transparent. They had no previous experience with plexiglass tables. They saw the abyss opening before them. They guessed they might fall. At the same time, the surface they touched seemed solid and continued over the abyss. They hesitated, then looked at their mothers' faces. If the mother was calm, they usually continued over the transparent part. If she seemed alarmed, they stopped and cried.[6]

The desire to seek companions and the tendency to adjust to their understanding of reality is also observable in adults. It was for instance tested experimentally by Lommen, Engelhard and Hout. About two months after deployment to Afghanistan, 213

Dutch soldiers were interviewed about stressful events that happened during their mission. They were told about a missile attack on their base on New Year's Eve. The event was described in some detail: the sound of the explosion, sightings of gravel projected just after the explosion. About seven months later, the soldiers were interviewed again. They were given a questionnaire about various types of events which included the missile attack. About a quarter of participants reported having experienced the attack. But the event was completely fictional.[7] The reports could only translate the soldiers' desire to be, like their comrades, at the heart of the action, their fear to be left behind, and their tendency to accept as true and real what the companions say happened.

This drive is so powerful that people even anticipate the thoughts of other people they regard as companions, or that they intend to approach as potential companions. It was observed in both infants and adults.

Experimenters showed infants and adults a cartoon with very simple scenes in which a ball may roll behind a wall, or out of the screen, or roll out of the screen and return. A character was present but could not always follow the ball and sometimes seemed to ignore its real destination. The adult spectators needed a little more time on average to indicate the ball's actual position when the character searched in the wrong direction, including when the character left the screen, as if the spectators took into account the motives they attributed to the character, which conflicted with the their own deductions about the position of the ball. The experimenters considered that the infants also paid attention to the character's thoughts because they stared at the screen longer when the character searched in the wrong direction[8].

Likewise, Sechrist and Stangor conducted an experiment to observe whether participants would indeed take into account the opinion expressed by peers. They did. The researchers evaluated with a survey the degree of racial prejudice in students on an American campus. The participants were later invited to debrief. They were told either that their peers concurred with them or that they did not. Finally a meeting with the other participants was organized. For each level of racism detected in the survey, the participants who had been told they were significantly more racist than their peers sat closer to a person from another "race" than the students with a similar level of racism who had not been told so. The opposite was observed for students who had been told that the other participants were neither more nor less racist than they were. The opinion attributed to peers reinforced personal opinion when it was convergent and weakened it when it was divergent.[9] And the students felt they had to comply with the opinion of their peers. In fact, self-judgments can be observed to be correlated to the opinions expressed by peers, just like judgments about other people.[10]

Once people have identified companions, they synchronize and adjust to their worldview. Other people do not elicit the same response. The mind is perfectly capable of making the distinction between companions and ordinary people.

For example, in San Pedro Manrique the spectators who were not friends or relatives of fire-walkers did not synchronize their heartbeats with them.[11] Likewise, the thoughts of people deemed repellent or unworthy of imitation are not imagined.[12] Once again, the quest for heroism does not imply general empathy.

The desire for companions is embedded into a desire to distinguish good from evil. It leads to imagine a bipolarization. Companions are always imagined to be opposed to adversaries who are assumed to do evil and to be manipulated by the Enemy.

Empathy is limited to companions. People project themselves into a bipolar world. Good is distinguished from evil. Companions are distinguished from all other people.

This explains that people experience pleasure when the people they consider companions and allies – for instance their sports teams – win and when their adversaries lose. They experience pain when the opposite happens, when their allies lose and their adversaries win. It is possible to observe specific neuronal responses for pleasure and for pain. These observations correspond to the feelings people report.[13]

The capacity to imagine two opposed sides is observable even in infants. Such beliefs are structural.

A recent experiment has indeed shown that this tendency was observable at a much earlier age than previously expected. Indeed, it can be illustrated by the reactions of six- and ten-month-old infants during an experiment based on a silent puppet show. The puppets were simply bright-colored shapes on sticks and with eyes: a triangle, a square and a circle. One of the puppets tried to climb a green slope, falling down again and again. The other two puppets intervened, one pushing the climber up the hill, the other pushing it down. After the show, infants were given the possibility to reach for either the helper or the hinderer and were much more likely to choose the helper.

During a last scene, the climber was placed between the helper and the hinderer. It went either to the helper or the hinderer. The infants looked longer at the scene if it went to the hinderer. It is likely that the infants interpreted the scenes like the adult experimenters did: although the objects were composed of extremely simple shapes, with as few details as possible to connect them with actual people, the infants spontaneously attributed to them distinct and opposed intentions. They also spontaneously preferred joining the helpers. They were surprised when the climber chose differently, which explains why they looked longer: they were thinking about a different option – going for the helper.[14]

This experiment confirmed the early development of linked tendencies: the tendency to imagine wills behind movements and to recognize faces even in objects, provided they remotely look like faces; the tendency to seek companions; the tendency to imagine their thoughts; the tendency to associate companions with a bipolar conflict; and the tendency to be taken aback when companions do not comply with that vision.

The more people find companions, the more they are self-confident and trusting of their intimate intuitions about good and evil. The more companions, the more people are mobilized, committed to a course of action, the more they reach out to new companions. The dynamic is accelerating.

10. Telling Friends from Foes

A heroic destiny is always present at the back of our minds. It shapes our vision of the world and, directly or indirectly, every idea. Nothing can disprove it. Even when our lives seem as disconnected as can be from heroic circumstances, the mind is still supremely attracted by these thoughts. Rather than to renounce them, the mind deduces the only possible explanation for the apparent disconnection between imagination and perception: the Enemy voluntarily hides. He secretly manipulates his victims because it enhances his powers. But then, how to be certain not to be in turn manipulated, and made to fight the wrong side?

Self-doubt makes its victims find themselves isolated, weakened and paralyzed. To tell right from wrong, companions are needed. They alone can tell the truth. The more people find companions, the more they are self-confident, the more they believe they can identify their real adversaries.

People who seem to act alone are often considered possessed by evil ideas. People who feel suddenly isolated tend to blame themselves and turn against themselves. Some people seem willing to act alone nonetheless. They do not care to verify if the ideas that they nurture are shared or not. In fact they have gotten used to not being followed by others. They tend to believe that the Enemy is so powerful that nobody else but them has detected him yet. However, having gotten used to not being taken seriously, they often display a bipolar behavior:

they are torn between a tendency to blame the others and an opposite tendency to consider their isolation as the sign that they are really possessed by evil ideas. They typically alternate between periods of hyperactivity and periods of depression. These bipolar cycles recede as soon as companions are found.

The expression of fellowship is enough to allow someone who was fearful and self-doubting to act boldly and with self-confidence.

A Royal Navy officer recalled an anecdote from his first battle at the turn of the nineteenth century. He was about to attack a vessel and was standing in the pinnace while the sailors were rowing. The enemy opened fire at the pinnace and the young officer felt "overpowered by fear." A senior officer, Lieutenant Ball, moved beside him. Without losing sight of the enemy vessel, he took the narrator's hand and encouraged him: "courage my dear Boy! Don't be afraid of yourself! You will recover in a minute or so – I was just the same when I first went out this way." The narrator soon felt better, understanding that he was "not yet dishonored."[1] The young officer had found a companion: someone who could understand his doubts and fears. Lieutenant Ball helped overcome those doubts and fears by offering to share a vision of victory. Such words from companions relieve people from self-doubt and fears. They are needed for a commitment to a course of action.

Self-doubt directly comes from the fear of being helpless and manipulated by the Enemy. This is why self-doubt is often accompanied by self-blame. One sees oneself as a servant of the Enemy. Only fellowship allows distinguishing good from evil. It takes a companion, someone that has been a victim too, and that one can help, to accept that one may not be a culprit that deserves a misfortune. Only a companion can confirm this version and help one to stop blaming oneself.

Here is an exemplar case: in 1992, a young woman, Barbara, was diagnosed with AIDS. She thought she would die within months, and anticipated her little boy would soon be an orphan. Her boyfriend, Antoine, confessed he had contaminated her. He said he had known he was ill but had been too ashamed, and too afraid of being rejected if she discovered the truth. Barbara plunged into depression but after a few months recovered enough to work as a waitress. She had another lover. When Antoine learned about the affair, he beat her. She moved away but they stayed in touch. She learned he was in a relationship. She asked him if he had protected sex. She did not get a clear reply and decided to warn the other woman. Antoine got again in a fury and threatened to kill her. Suddenly realizing that she might not be the only one to have been contaminated by her ex-boyfriend, she started feeling hatred for him. She started considering herself a victim rather than a culprit.

Before that, she had been possessed by the idea that she had committed a fault and had focused on living on, for the sake of her child and of her boyfriend. This had not been easy. A high-level consumption of drugs and alcohol had marked the previous years. A suicide attempt raised little compassion in her family. But now, she understood differently. Instead of focusing only on fighting off the virus, she also felt she had to do something to protect the other victims, actual or potential. She decided to sue her ex-boyfriend. The case was dismissed. But together with other women Barbara then formed an association, to help victims and raise awareness about their plight. It took several years before a judge decided to hand down a guilty verdict. Barbara declared she was proud of the part she had played in fighting not only the virus but also domestic violence.[2]

Finding companions, other victims that she could help, allowed Barbara to move from blaming herself alongside her former lover and doubting herself, to blaming only her contaminator and other violent men.

Fellowship, the expression of friendship, sympathy or solidarity in the face of common adversaries, is the condition to be self-confident, to trust that one acts rightfully. Conversely, isolation is interpreted as a sign of madness, an indicator that someone may possesses evil ideas.

In 2013, Alex Jones joined David Aaronovitch on *BBC UK* to discuss the annual conference of the Bilderberg Group, a prestigious think tank that gathers, among others, chairpersons of major international groups and senior members of national governments. Jones explained he was there to reveal that Bilderberg was a secret Nazi organization which had imposed the Euro to take over the government of the European countries. Aaronovitch acknowledged his own skepticism and replied "you are a lone crusader powering against them, so how come you're still alive – one, they don't exist, two, you're part of the conspiracy. I say the first… It's happened in your head."[3]

Being isolated is assimilated with being mad. As a consequence, people who cannot find companions and feel isolated tend to spontaneously turn against themselves and blame themselves.

I observed such a case a few years ago during a seminar organized by Welsh language activists for a group of fellow European linguists. Our host was describing with rising indignation the oppression of Welsh inhabitants by English immigrants. His monologue took place just after lunch while the other participants were resting, feeling drowsy and listening in silence, barely nodding at his words. Suddenly he realized the situation, interrupted his speech and apologized with marked embarrassment: "Sorry, I'm getting emotional." He blamed himself for the discrepancy between his own exaltation and the relative apathy of his public.

Isolated people turn against themselves because the search for an adversary endures, even when one is isolated. They have no one else to turn against. However, since isolation also generates self-doubt and hinders action, they are more likely to turn against themselves violently soon after being isolated. The likelihood of violent action decreases with time.

This point is well illustrated by the occurrence of suicides in prison. They are more frequent just after contacts with the outside world: a visit, the receipt of news, especially of bad news like a divorce, or even after a feast such as Christmas, which acts as a reminder of the outside world. Such circumstances renew the impetus to attack oneself. The probability of suicide attempts following such events decreases with time, a clear sign that isolation also engenders demobilization.[4]

If isolation engenders self-doubt, prolonged self-doubt also hinders the development of new ties of fellowship, in a vicious circle. People who have gotten used to not being followed by others tend to believe that the Enemy is so powerful and manipulative that no one else is aware of his presence. They are torn between a tendency to blame others for not understanding the truth and an opposite tendency to consider their isolation as the sign that they are really possessed by evil ideas.

Such behavior could be observed in the case of General William T. Sherman in 1861, when he was assigned to the command of the Army of Cumberland during the early stages of the American Civil War. After a reconnaissance into the countryside, he wrote to his Commander-in-Chief that the enemy was conspiring to create a "vast force" that would soon "overwhelm" his regiment.

His conclusions alarmed his peers and superiors. However, they could find no sign of the "vast force" that Sherman had detected. Sherman himself provided no further evidence as if he did not hope to convince anyone. He seemed unable to reach out. Actually, he appeared incapable of listening to anyone either, and "talked incessantly," unable to halt the obsessive train of thoughts he nurtured. He was displaying all kinds of signs of an extreme nervousness. He barely slept for weeks.

The apparent apathy of his peers reinforced his fears that the enemy could not be resisted. He felt that no one was even attempting to mobilize the necessary forces. He constantly suspected betrayal. But at the same time, this understanding did not make him feel more in charge. Sherman actually displayed an acute lack of self-confidence; he felt particularly incapable of leading his men and asked repeatedly to be relieved from his command. His vision of an all-powerful and manipulative enemy not only implied lack of confidence in others but also in himself. In letters addressed to his wife, he acknowledged: "I find myself riding a whirlwind unable to guide the storm." In the near future he anticipated total "failure and humiliation," an onrushing infamy that "nearly makes me crazy — indeed I may be so now."[5]

Sherman's conduct can be described as learned self-helplessness. Throughout his professional life Sherman had learned, unwillingly, to expect defeat. He had "careened from failure to failure..."[6] Contrary to General Grant, Sherman had not been involved in any major action during the Mexican-American War. A commander in California, he struggled to keep his troops from deserting for the gold mines. This first disgrace was followed by another when his company went bankrupt in 1857 in spite of the powerful backing of his family. The first year of the Civil War seemed to confirm this seemingly endless series of misfortunes. Sherman resigned the presidency of the Louisiana military academy, then took command of a brigade at Bull Run that retreated in disorder in the face of the Confederate assault.

Although Sherman and his wife identified previous failures as the cause of his depression, he could not help but consider himself a loser. Someone who would have been more acquainted with success and to enlisting companions and allies would have tried harder to present and discuss a workable strategy, which would have meant subduing feelings about the Enemy's forces, which would in turn ultimately serve as a reality check. Sherman was overwhelmed by a sense of helplessness. He actually reached out for help. But his extreme, unrestricted, vision of the Enemy, which was of course both the consequence of his isolation and the source of his distress, could not be shared by less depressed people.

Sherman was eventually sent home for several weeks, after which he was assigned a new commander, General Ulysses S. Grant. This meeting changed him completely. Contrary to his previous superiors, Grant sympathized with Sherman's psychological plight. He took his requests into account and assigned Sherman to a subordinate command. This mark of understanding created a bond between them. Sherman soon regained a little self-confidence. During the terrible Battle of Shiloh on April 6-7, 1862, his bravery and tactical skills were recognized by Grant who offered him a major command soon after. Meeting with General Grant transformed Sherman from a "self-proclaimed looser... to the confident and brilliantly creative commander..."[7] Their relation throughout the Civil War is a good example of the dynamics engendered by fellowship.

People need companions to gain self-confidence and get mobilized. In most cases, people know how to reach out and find fellowship. But this essential skill may be unlearned when repeated failures confine someone into believing that nothing can be done. Yet, even in such cases, fellowship may re-induce a state of mind where cooperation and learning from one another is possible.

Fellowship and isolation trigger radical shifts in the perception of events, the course of action and in the level of mobilization. These radical shifts can only be explained by the binary mode of thinking implied by the heroic scenario. One can only be either fighting evil or fighting for the Enemy. There is no third way.

11.Converging Visions of History

Each one recognizes only two camps: companions and adversaries. All adversaries are considered to belong to a single camp, whatever their differences. Indeed, they must all ultimately serve the Enemy, the unique source of all evils. In turn, all the adversaries of the adversaries are imagined to belong to a single camp, because they all ultimately fight the Enemy. Each one imagines a bipolar confrontation.

This vision tends to become real. Indeed, each one can only imagine that the Enemy voluntarily hides. He must secretly manipulate his victims. Secrecy must enhance his powers. To fight him implies to force him to reveal himself. Provocations are necessary to make his agents react and betray themselves. Actions are therefore designed to provoke adversaries, to make them reveal their true nature, to make them commit evil in return.

Provocations often elicit righteous reactions, which are partly modeled on the original provocations, the better to counter them. In turn, the original aggressors find themselves vindicated by the hostile reactions they have triggered and may find renewed inspiration in them. As a result, from reaction to reaction, interacting people become increasingly aware of mutual hostility and also aware of alliances. Two hostile coalitions build up.

The more events evoke the heroic scenario, with a clear and neat distinction between good and evil, the more people mobilize and interact with each other. The more people find companions and adversaries, the more they are mobilized, and the more they can reach out to new companions. The general dynamics of bipolarization accelerates.

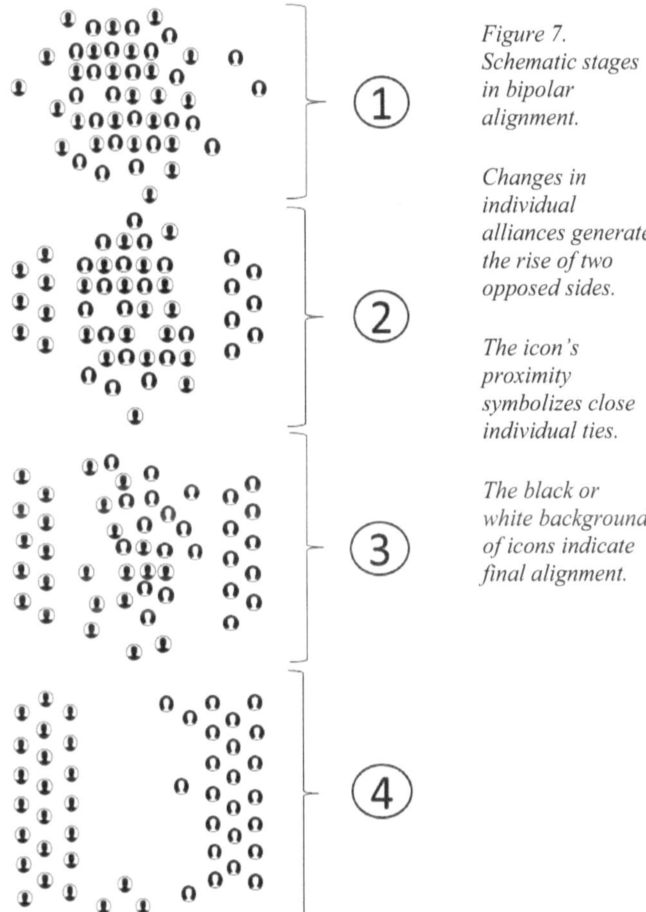

Figure 7. Schematic stages in bipolar alignment.

Changes in individual alliances generate the rise of two opposed sides.

The icon's proximity symbolizes close individual ties.

The black or white background of icons indicate final alignment.

Both sides thus also converge on a new vision of History. This new vision of History is deemed by both sides to be the true, revealed History. The sole difference between both visions tends to be that events deemed positive by one side are considered negatively by the other.

A bipolarization could not take place without provocations. Without such moves, multiple reactions could not take place. If any action was merely a proportional reaction, there could be no acceleration in the interactions, no escalation in hostilities. Although each action is always justified as a proportional reaction, it cannot be so in reality.

Most provocations are considered ridicule "conspiracy theories." Even when they attract a little attention, their authors are usually seen as lone psychics. However, not all fail to elicit reactions. A few gain enough attention and adhesion to ultimately generate vast bipolar mobilizations. Some even inspire world wars.

The Protocols of the Elders of Zion (1903) is one of the best-known conspiracy theories. The *Protocols* presents itself as a transcript of the minutes of a secret meeting that happened in the late nineteenth century. They were supposed to reveal a Jewish plan to destroy the traditional Christian social order and achieve global domination.

Most commentators are eager to establish its lack of authenticity. They note that it was published anonymously and contained remarkably few specifics. It is impossible to identify the participants in the meeting: the "minutes" used almost exclusively the first-person plural, and mentioned only very general goals like controlling global finance, the media, etc. Furthermore, the early versions of the *Protocols* contained mutually-contradicting details: one was peppered with French words, the other with a reference to a Zionist meeting that took place in Russia, etc.[1]

It is likely that the *Protocols* was inspired by previous fictional works, most of which had been published with a view to evoke real politics and denounce real events under the guise of fiction.

One of the most direct sources of inspiration was probably Hermann Goedsche's 1868 *Biarritz,* which presents a narration of a midnight secret meeting of the Twelve Tribes of Israel in presence of the Devil himself in the Jewish Cemetery in Prague.[2]

It is also likely that the authors never sought to produce a credible document in the first place. They viewed their creation as a provocation. They actually wanted it to be easily recognized as inauthentic by unsympathetic readers. They wanted it to elicit reactions; the more outraged the reactions, the better. However, the authors did not believe the text in and of itself was sufficient to elicit the desired outrage. So they published it within the context of pogroms during which thousands of Jews fled Russia or were killed. It is likely that the authors actually participated in these pogroms themselves. And they hoped that the global outrage caused by the pogroms would attach itself to their forgery. They succeeded.

The document was indeed denounced as a forgery on various occasions. It was even declared "harmful" and "laughable nonsense" by a Swiss Court in 1906. These denunciations gave the text a global publicity. Denunciations and rebuttals then served as arguments to the *Protocols* proponents. Anti-Semites saw them as the best proof that, whatever the authenticity of the documents, its contents reflected a real plan: why would powerful media need to denounce a forgery if it did not contain real, valuable information? Did not Henry Ford himself have to apologize and close his newspaper after having published the *Protocols*? [3]

Whether they had really been drafted by Russian *agents provocateurs* mattered little. In the eyes of its supporters, the publication had served its goal: make the Enemy's agents react and betray themselves. This was, for instance, Hitler's point of view in *Mein Kampf*. This is why the Nazi regime paid little attention to the *Protocols* in the late 1930s, when the document had been so important early on. The Nazis felt the document, true or forged, had played its role and helped reveal to the world the Jewish threat. Once they had control on the German state apparatus, there was no need to perpetuate obsolete debates. What was a necessary provocation early on had become unnecessary if not counter-productive a few years later.

The global threat that the *Protocols* was supposed to reveal reflected a set of beliefs which, marginal and absurd as it must have seemed to many observers early on, concurred to the rise of radical movements such as Nazism, and, as such, to the bipolarization which led to World War II. It still holds sway nowadays, notably with movements such as Hamas.

The early success of the text was not due to its authenticity but to the characteristic evocation of the Enemy: a secret, hidden will bent on dominating the whole world through a series of moves designed to ruin the natural order. The text's vagueness, far from being a weakness, was on the contrary the key to its global dissemination. As such, it illustrates well the dynamics of conspiracy theories. Almost all of them seem to be the product of isolated, deranged authors. Yet some eventually help nourish large bipolar mobilizations.

It might first seem especially incoherent that the authors of such provocations on the one hand knew perfectly well of their forgery and on the other, still believed that the threat was real. In fact, their actions only make sense if provocations were deemed necessary because the Enemy himself wanted to stay hidden. Far from being a problem, provocations indicate the action logic. Provocations are deemed necessary to ultimately undo evil. While they would otherwise be deemed excessive, they are considered appropriate to defeat the Enemy.

The dissemination of false news was justified that way in 1989 Czechoslovakia. The fall of the Communist regime was prompted by massive demonstrations eight days after the fall of the Berlin Wall. Demonstrators answered a rumor that a nineteen-year-old university student named Martin Smid had been brutally killed by the police. The journalist Jan Urban, helped disseminate the news. He later called it "a professional blunder" because it was a false rumor and he had believed it true at the time. But he also justified the publication as a way to "wake a nation out of its collective apathy" and prompt the rising against Communism. It was the event, according to him, that put an end to the "deal" between the Communist government and the people: "You shut up and we will take care of you." It revealed the brutality of the regime.[4]

The assassination of the Archduke Franz Ferdinand of Austria by Gavrilo Princip, on June 28, 1914, in Sarajevo was also a typical provocation (Figure 8).

The murderer did not have a personal reason to take revenge against the Archduke; the murder was not in itself deemed a way to end evil, in that case the occupation of the Southern Slav territories by Austria-Hungary; it was merely viewed as an act that could trigger a war between Serbia and Austria-Hungary and thus a world war through international alliances: Russia was believed to be committed to defending Serbia against Austria-Hungary, which in turn would drag all major world powers into the conflict. The war was hoped to lead to the demise of the Austrian-Hungarian Empire and thus to the liberation of the Southern Slavs.

Figure 8. The assassination of Franz Ferdinand (Le Petit Journal, July 12, 1914). [5]

Another example of a successful provocation, one that triggered a series of hostile reactions, albeit on a more limited scale, could be observed on October 14, 2014, during a soccer match between the national teams of Serbia and Albania. The chain reaction started when a small drone was flown low over the stadium, trailing a banner that read "Greater Albania," the territory that would result from the reunification of Albania with Kosovo, a province also claimed by many Serbian nationalists as their own. The banner was emblazoned with the word "autochthonous," a reference to the claim that Albanians descended from the original people living in the Balkans, the ancient Illyrians, while the Serbs descended from Slavic invaders and therefore had no right to govern the Albanians. Serbian fans immediately reacted by booing and whistling before chanting, "Kill! Kill! Kill!" The banner was dropped close to the field, and a Serbian player took it. He was immediately accosted by Albanian players who were in turn attacked by a Serbian supporter armed with a chair. The English referee then decided to suspend the game, and the players ran from the field. A video posted online showed a crowd of Albanians responding in kind to the chant they earlier heard in Belgrade: "Kill! Kill! Kill Serbs!" Albania's youth minister claimed that the players had been welcomed as heroes in Tirana, the Albanian capital.[6] The rapidity and importance of the reactions can only be explained by the familiarity of the people with the History associated with the banner, a result of the 1999 conflict in Kosovo between Serbs and Albanians. Reactions are typically modeled on previous moves by the other side.

A bipolarization is characterized by the presence of two sides that have come to recognize each other as opponents. They tend to react increasingly to each other's moves, to denounce them and to adjust their own actions in order to better counter the opponent's moves. Both sides believe that the other is deliberately misleading the other and seems less dangerous than it really is; they see no reason to seek compromise but try on the contrary to gather arguments and support in order to compensate their supposed inferiority and vulnerability. People need not be backed by many supporters to feel legitimate to act; they need only to react to the moves of the other side.

Such a limited configuration could be observed in contemporary Japan regarding the way history schoolbooks deal with World War II and the treatment of the populations occupied by the Japanese army. The "Nanking Massacre" or "The Rape of Nanking" in particular happens to focus attention and generate opposed views.

One side argues that the Japanese Army did nothing wrong. Its leading figure, Nobukatsu Fujioka, one of the most active authors on the issue, considers that the Chinese government fabricated evidence and hired actors. On the other side, Tamaki Matsuoka argues that the massacre was no forgery. She claims she interviewed 250 Japanese soldiers who "admitted to killing, stealing and raping."

Disagreement also concerns other aspects of Japanese military activities during World War II such as the Korean "comfort women" used by the Japanese army. Fujioka believes they were paid prostitutes. His opponent considers them sex slaves.

Nobukatsu Fujioka wants to see references to events such as the Nanking Massacre or comfort women suppressed from textbooks. On the contrary, Tamaki Matsuoka believes that the textbooks pay far too much attention to ancient times and not enough to recent events such as World War II, so that most Japanese students are actually unaware of the importance of events that cause so much resentment in China and Korea. She considers this deliberate: that people in the Japanese ministry did not really believe in the official doctrine which professes that textbooks must treat historical events involving neighboring Asian countries fairly.[7]

Nobukatsu Fujioka and Tamaki Matsuoka have recognized each other as adversaries for more than a decade. Although Matsuoka received threats from nationalist groups when her book was published, the argument between both authors did not receive much public attention during the 2000s. Then, in 2013, Shinzo Abe, Japan's Prime Minister, sided with Fujioka and castigated the curriculum as "anti-Japanese."[8] He moved on the issue in a time of renewed Sino-Japanese tensions. Both countries were contesting sovereignty over the East China Sea.

A bipolarization may thus at first mobilize intensely only a few people over a long time, before engulfing a much greater number.

From provocation to reaction, both sides tend to align their actions, and the justifications that support them. The bipolar mobilization triggers a convergence in the visions of History. Such a convergence took place for example during the Cold War, a major period of international bipolarization analyzed by Hannah Arendt. The vision of history of the defenders of the United States converged with the one propagated by the defenders of the Soviet Union.

In 1945, the Allies, led by the United States, Great Britain and the Soviet Union, defeated the Axis, led by Germany and Japan. From that point on, US policy makers increasingly tended to view the Soviet Union as a new global threat. The Soviet Union indeed claimed to unite the adversaries of the United States under its aegis.

It was increasingly assumed that the Soviet leadership was coherent, centralized and perfectly determined to achieve global domination. It was often referred to simply as "Moscow." Equally, it was increasingly believed that many communist agents were hidden in neighboring countries, manipulating naïve authorities, weakening them and making their population easier to conquer. It was as if the Soviet leadership was playing a game of dominoes. Countries seemed to fall to communism one after another[9]

As a result, US intelligence reports that denied Soviet leadership in popular movements were discarded, especially in countries that the Soviet Union proclaimed it would add to the growing communist bloc. Skeptical reports were seen as engineered by Soviet secret services to mislead the US. The case of Vietnam was typical: reports underlining the local nature of the communist movement were ignored. So were sources that mentioned Sino-Vietnamese tensions. Hannah Arendt observed that requests for assistance from Ho Chi Minh, the Vietnamese communist leader, who sought to counterbalance Soviet influence in Vietnam, were simply left without answers.[10]

As a consequence of the identification of Moscow with the Enemy, the US government tended to align its methods of government on those of the Soviet Union: both regimes converged. On the internal front, the growing obsession with the communist threat weakened trust in elective democracy and in the traditional US government, even though the US Constitution was deemed to be the foundation of the American way of life and of the opposition to Moscow. Indeed, the US government itself was increasingly perceived as excessively open to external influences and manipulations. A large campaign of denunciation and exclusion of "communist spies" was launched, not unlike the contemporary purges in the Soviet Union, albeit with less deadly consequences; indeed, the Soviet killing machine was little known at the time and could not be fully emulated.

On the external front, it was believed that if Moscow's advance was left unchecked, no country could stay immune from communism forever. The United States could not opt again for isolationism but must, as the most distant nation from Moscow and the most immune from communist influence, lead the resistance by building another block, the "Free World." This was the basis of the "containment" and "roll back" strategies that aimed to counter communist forces in neighboring nations and, whenever it was possible, to reconquer fallen countries. Peoples' right to free-determination, hitherto the principle of the US policy, was regarded with growing suspicion. Although Kennedy vowed not to impose a "Pax Americana," an American authoritarian protectorate on allied countries, the US policy increasingly tended in that direction, just like the Soviet policy did.[11]

This bipolar convergence in policy-making strengthened the Soviet Bloc as much as the Free World. Ho Chi Minh, for example, was left by the United States with no alternative than to turn exclusively to Moscow for help. The bipolar convergence left non-aligned countries with fewer opportunities and helped the expansion of the two blocks.

*

Aaron T. Beck observed that the notion of a powerful, hidden and manipulative Enemy was the cause that made people in a group impervious to counter-argument. Since "they view their Enemy as using all available tools of deception, any disconfirming evidence is interpreted as proof of the Enemy's deceptions." Beck named this dynamic "groupthink."[12] He observed that in such groups, people never question what their companions say. They simply accept it as the truth.

However, even if the group of companions tends to discredit any other point of view, it is not isolated but pays much attention to the messages and actions from other groups, especially hostile ones. It adapts to these signals and "employs counterstrategies of stealth and subversion to counteract the invisible as well as the overt manipulations of the Enemy."[13]

Beck failed to recognize that these tendencies are not "abnormal." Some of their manifestations may have seemed "extreme" in the United States during the 1990s, such as the Waco Sect or the patriotic militias.[14] But they cannot be corrected and cured. People cannot understand for instance that their sense of vulnerability is misplaced.[15] Beck did not distinguish between the capacity of the therapist to help willing couples stop fighting, and his capacity to put an end, for instance, to a civil war in which neither side desires to be stopped on the path towards what they believe will be victory. Beck thus fails to see that aggression cannot generally be corrected; people are not reasonable. Empathy, the desire to share in someone else's feelings, ideas and destiny, is proper to fellowship and therefore cannot be separated from hostility for other people.

The groups described by Beck are not "abnormal" either in the statistical sense. The growth of such groups, and their transformation into large national or international coalitions, can be observed throughout history. In the process, all became less secretive, more open about their goals, and no less convinced of the need to fight the Enemy. The dynamics at hand are best captured by the term "bipolarization."

Clausewitz was the first to produce a complete description of bipolarization as the "law" of conflicts[16]. He isolated its causes and recognized that hostility was a general tendency; "even the most civilized nations may burn with passionate hatred of each other,"[17] especially when they can find inspiration in the history of previous conflicts.

Clausewitz identified the precise bipolar nature of all conflicts: the conflict shapes two hostile sides.[18] He explained the dynamic nature of the process. The reciprocal reactions generate an acceleration. These tendencies can always be observed: "the more violent the excitement which precedes the war… so much more will it be directed to the destruction of the Enemy…"[19] Furthermore, reactions generate a convergence in the acceleration. Both sides know that if they "desire to defeat the enemy, [they] must proportion [their] efforts to his powers of resistance… but the adversary does the same, therefore, there is a new mutual enhancement, which, in pure conception, must create a fresh effort towards an extreme."[20]

12. The International Bipolarization

People believe only the facts that are confirmed by companions and by the reactions of their common adversaries. As both sides build up they converge not only on the causes of the conflict, but also on the way the battles should be fought and on the conditions of victory and defeat. Thus, when the conflict reaches its most intense phase, both sides can agree, in spite of extreme mutual hostility, that one was victorious and the other one was defeated. They stop fighting. Bipolarization thus peaks with the victory of one side and the defeat of the other.

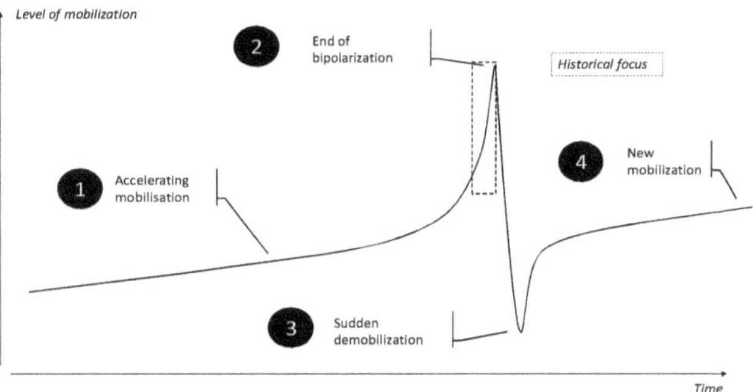

Figure 9. The bipolarization cycle.

The event is followed by a general demobilization, as both sides suddenly lack the adversary they were accustomed to. Bipolarization is a cyclical process. It accelerates, then peaks and decelerates (*Figure 9*).

However, the victory does not signal the advent of the new golden age the fighters had imagined. It merely signals the end of one cycle of bipolarization and the beginning of another.

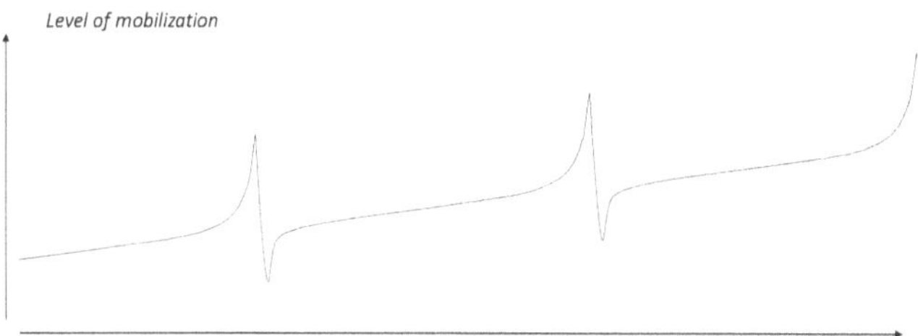

Figure 10. Bipolarization cycles.

Conflicts are cyclical (*Figure 10*). Alternative hypotheses are simply not observed. There is nowhere a permanent "war of all against all,"[1] nor a permanent peace.

Most of the time the level of conflict seems very low. Compared to the phases of intense conflict, there seems to be almost no conflict at all. This impression is reinforced by a binary distinction between periods of "peace" and periods of "war" that are present in most historical accounts. Historians make wars seemingly "break out" in the middle of peaceful relations, which allows them to underline the peaceful intentions of one side and the deceitfulness of the other side.

Historians tend to focus on the comparatively short periods of intense conflict. These periods are when history is the most intensely rewritten, and the ones which tend to draw attention even long after they are over (*Figure 9*).

The events that take place during one cycle condition the development of the next cycles. Bipolarization is a dynamic that unfolds over many cycles. Over the very long term, it shapes an international history and an international society.

The history produced over a cycle of bipolarization is not suddenly forgotten because the conflict ends. The narrative is passed on. People inherit from previous cycles a history that they deplore or take pride in. They also inherit allies and adversaries that they cannot change at will. Even when peace has been declared, previous adversaries continue to view each other as the Enemy. Peace, in most cases, can be no more than a truce. It may sometimes last, however, in spite of all the accumulated distrust, but on one condition only: that previous adversaries recognize a new, more dangerous adversary. This may be for instance the case if a previous adversary appears so much weakened by the defeat and a previous ally so much reinforced by the victory that the former ally, rather than the former adversary, now appears as the most dangerous foe, the real Enemy.

The initiative of an alliance always belongs to the victors, not to the vanquished. In that respect, it is true that history is written by the victors. The vanquished are driven to doubt themselves. They suspect that their vision of history was misleading and that some of them at least were serving the real Enemy. They tend to turn against each other. If the victors accept to enter into an alliance with the vanquished, the side that supports this option among the vanquished takes over. It is vindicated by the attitude of the victors. If the victors do not propose an alliance to the vanquished, the side that seeks revenge is vindicated and takes over.

These dynamics are typically reflected by the alliances and conflicts between the great powers of the twentieth century. Each alliance and conflict was the result of the worldview that emerged during the previous periods of conflict.

In the nineteenth century, France was considered by Britain as the most dangerous power on the European continent. This changed after 1870 and the defeat of France by Germany, and even more so after 1890 when the new German Empire set out to outcompete Britain as a world power. From that point on, France became an acceptable ally against Germany, and so did

Russia, another major competitor on the European scene and a previous adversary. Britain, who had defeated both France and Russia during the nineteenth century, took the initiative of offering both these countries an alliance against Germany. During the war with Germany, Britain was also able to enlist Japan, China, Italy and the USA. The war was thus remembered as the First World War (1914-1918).

Germany was defeated in 1918, but not before it defeated Russia and made a separate peace with Russia, which transformed into the Soviet Union. As a result, over the following years, the Russian-dominated Soviet Union did not appear as a threat that justified an alliance with Germany in France or in Britain, let alone in the United States. Although the Soviets had vowed to carry out a worldwide revolution, the defeat of Russia by Germany in 1918 at a time when Germany was also facing France, Britain and the USA on another front, convinced the victors that the Soviets were not a danger that warranted an alliance with Germany. In effect, they continued to act as if Germany was still the main threat.

And so they prepared, unwittingly, a new conflict with Germany and allowed her to enlist not only the Soviet Union but also disgruntled former allies like Italy and Japan. Indeed, France, Britain and the US had not accepted key demands of Italy and Japan. Many Italians and Japanese considered that their countries had not been treated fairly by the peace treaties. They prevailed and prepared a revenge against the most senior victorious powers: France and Britain. During the 1930s, they joined the vanquished nations, Germany and the Soviet Union, which had each emerged from a civil war. Together, they started World War II as a revenge against France and Britain.

In 1941, confident of a victory against France and Britain, Germany and Italy turned against Russia, which immediately sided with Britain, France and later, the United States. Together these countries vanquished Italy, Germany and Japan in 1945.

The appreciation of the balance of powers changed completely during World War II when it appeared that a massively weakened Soviet Union was still capable of pushing back and of defeating Germany and its allies.

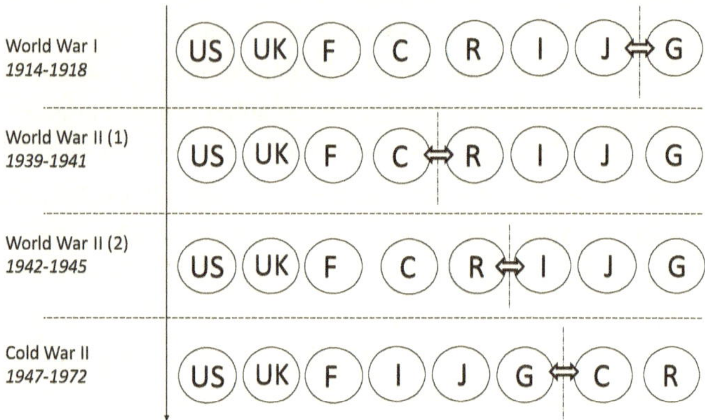

Figure 11. The alignment of great powers in 20th-century world wars.

US: the United States of America; UK: the United Kingdom (Britain); F: France; C: China; R: Russia (Soviet Union after 1917); I: Italy; J: Japan; G: Germany.

In 1945 the Soviet Union thus replaced Germany, Italy and Japan as the principal threat in the eyes of the American, British and French. These powers accepted to ally themselves with their former adversaries. The US, Britain and France were careful to occupy a large part of Germany, which they remobilized after 1949 as a bulwark against the USSR. Germany, Italy and Japan had become acceptable allies against the Soviet threat, especially after the USSR had gained a major ally in the People's Republic of China in 1949 (Figure 11).

Former adversaries share a common vision of history. They are prepared to recognize each other as adversaries once more. But they can also recognize new common adversaries and become allies. Over successive periods of bipolarization, the probability of this second possibility increases. The coalitions thus tend to become larger. The history they share tends to encompass more nations. Over the very long term, an increasingly largely shared vision of history can thus come to define an expanding international society, a group of people who have come to recognize each other as worthy allies or adversaries.

An international society emerged and expanded in Europe from 1500 to 2000. It shared a common international history. And its advent was marked by increasingly large international coalitions.

In the sixteenth century, major conflicts opposed on average no more than two great powers. That number rose to four in the seventeenth century, to five in the eighteenth century and to more than seven in the twentieth century. Virtually all major powers were involved in each of the two World Wars (Figure 12). The total number of great powers in Europe did not change that much from 1500 to 2000, which means that over the period great powers felt they were less and less able to watch another conflict from the sidelines.

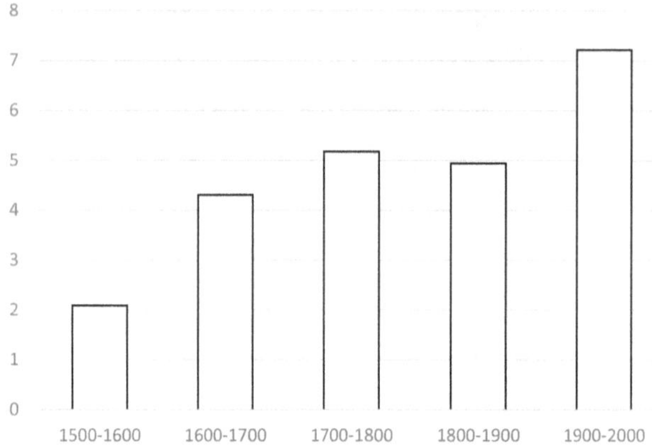

Figure 12. Average number of great powers involved in major conflicts in Europe (1500-2000).2

At the beginning of the period, European powers saw alliances and the balance of powers as something that was relatively fluid and changing. Over the next centuries, as an international history was increasingly shared, all became increasingly prepared to fear the rise of a group of competitors against which they had already been pitted in the past. The European powers increasingly anticipated future conflicts and shared converging visions of threats. To counter them, great powers became increasingly part of large coalitions. They were prepared to recognize that a victory of one side would benefit such a large coalition and would be so detrimental to the other one, that one could hardly stay neutral.

For example, during most of the sixteenth century, the two largest powers, the Kingdom of France and the Dutch-German-Spanish Empire of the Habsburgs, fought for pre-eminence. But the other powers, England, the Pope, Milan, Venice and Genoa regularly switched sides. By contrast, during the first half of the seventeenth century, the Habsburg and their allies, and the coalition that opposed them, remained very much the same. That pattern of stability in international coalitions was only to get more pronounced as European coalitions tended to encompass more powers over the next centuries.

Conflicts were originally much more frequent because they were much less synchronized. There had almost always been a war somewhere. However, the scale of early conflicts was quite limited compared with later ones. As they became more synchronized, wars occurred more rarely. But when war did occur, it happened on a scale unseen before, and engulfed many more nations. Mobilization became much more intense, and conflicts became much more devastating. This can be measured by the rising number of yearly fatalities relative to the total population in the course of these ever-more synchronized, short and generalized conflicts (Figure 13).

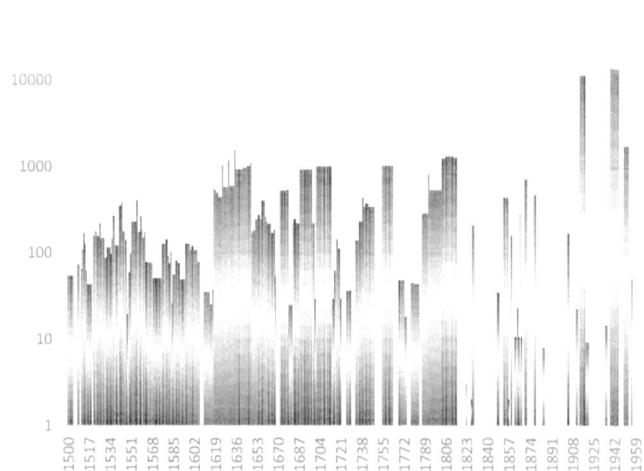

Figure 13. Annual battle fatalities in great powers wars per million European population, Europe, 1500-2000 (log scale).[3]

The history of Europe from 1500 to 2000 is plainly that of a continent where increasingly large coalitions and conflicts took shape, as people increasingly shared an international history and an international society. Bipolarization rose and generalized.

Bipolarization is ubiquitous. Any number of people in interaction tends to reproduce the same dynamics. Over many periods of bipolarization, the dynamics of convergence may transform very local events with little reference to a broader history, into the history of a whole international society.

The ubiquity of bipolarization may be illustrated by the "The Robbers' Cave Experiment," a summer camp organized and observed in June and July 1954 by a team of researchers led by Muzafer Sherif. The researchers selected boys who did not know each other previously, with average social background and school tests and no obvious cause for prejudice against each other. The boys were enlisted in two groups: the Eagles and the Rattlers,[4] but each group was left ignorant of the existence of the other group. They only got to know the other boys from their own group. After a few days the two groups were introduced to each other and immediately engaged against one another in competitions, involving, for instance, games of baseball and tug-of-war. All the boys expressed a strong dislike for the members of the other group. They were reluctant to share the same facilities and raided the other group's belongings. Derogative language and aggressive actions were directed towards the other group. But the boys of the group who had lost a game also expressed a dislike for the other boys in the same group and more frequently insisted on leaving the summer camp. On the contrary, winners did so much less frequently.

During the next phase, the organizers set up difficult tasks that necessitated the cooperation of both groups: fixing a water tank that vandals had supposedly damaged and pulling a broken truck. To pull the truck, the boys used the tug-of-war rope. They spontaneously imagined that together they had "won the tug-of-war against the truck."[5] The previous phases of opposition had provided the boys with a convergent vision of the adversary: the other side at a tug-of-war. This enabled them to "fight" alongside each other against their new adversary: the truck. They were happy to have defeated a common adversary together. Success immediately brought much better feelings towards the boys of the other group. During the last days of the summer camp, the boys played and shared activities regardless of previous group lines. The boys of The Robbers' Cave Experiment spontaneously produced group dynamics that can also be observed in international conflicts.

This illustrates the constant properties of bipolarization. It always produces the same dynamics, whatever the scale of conflict and alliances, or the specifics of the history. Of course, in the twentieth-century United States, few adults would have been as emotionally committed by the events at the summer camp as the boys. They would have dismissed the events as insignificant compared to the magnitude and complexity of conflicts like world wars. Their worldview was an international history many centuries long and covering the entire international society.

However, they had inherited that international history. This history had been passed and developed and made more complex over many generations. And originally, it was not more complex nor did it cover events that were on a much different scale than the events that took place in the Robbers' Cave Experiment.

Most of the historical events that have been passed on to us from seventh-century Britain seem indeed hardly less local than the events generated during the summer camp. They account only for the feats and battles of little bands of warriors with no reference to a wider historical context.[6] Centuries of conflicts and convergence completely transformed the worldview of these groups. The larger coalitions which were produced over time gradually aggregated territories into larger units and events into more complex narratives.

In seventh-century Britain, most infighting occurred between lords and groups who controlled territories no larger than the shires that would come later. In 800, the whole of England was already dominated by four kingdoms only: Northumbria, Mercia, East Anglia and Wessex. By 1000, England was one Kingdom. By 1200, it belonged to the Plantagenet Empire which also dominated Scotland, Ireland, Normandy, Brittany, Anjou and Aquitaine. It was a rival only to the Kingdom of France and the Germanic "Holy Roman Empire" in the domination of Western Europe. England is presently the largest nation of the United Kingdom, a state that is committed to long-term alliances in North America, Europe and Oceania. The international society to which it belongs covers the whole world.

However limited and local the apparent stakes, any conflict, any rivalry converges over the long term in a general bipolarization. Our international society and our international history are themselves the very-long-term result of such an international convergence.

13. From Personal Rivalries
to World War

The general bipolarization is fueled by personal alliances and rivalries. But as the general bipolarization rises, all alliances, rivalries and policies must either align or subside.

This is perfectly illustrated by the run-up to World War I. A bitter personal rivalry between the sovereigns of Britain and Germany fueled the conflict. Of all the policies, conflicts and rivalries that existed before the conflict and emerged during its acceleration, only those who appeared the most in touch with the Enemy's intentions prevailed. The other ones had to align or subside.

At the beginning of the 1890s few British would have regarded Germany as a threat. For three quarters of a century the security of Britain had been absolute, its supremacy unchallenged. Britain was an island. It did not have a large army. It did not need one. The Royal Navy alone could defend it. It surpassed all other navies put together. It had repeatedly demonstrated its capacity to defeat any naval power, including France and Russia. Britain could stand in "splendid isolation." It did not need anymore to commit itself to alliances on the continent. Europe was under a proper balance of powers; European nations were checking each other. The Royal Navy guaranteed

Britain unlimited access to a colonial empire that covered a quarter of all lands, and to trade routes with virtually any part of the world. No one could seemingly threaten its prosperity and indeed its domination of the world.

This sense of security was shattered in 1899, when Germany announced that it would build a navy to rival Britain's. Britain suddenly woke up to the fact that the balance of power had recently tilted far too much in Germany's favor. Germany had become the most powerful state on the European continent. It had the strongest economy and had the most efficient army. Should it be engaged in a continental war again, it would likely prevail and then control economic means far outstripping British ones. A German naval buildup could then outpace British capacities. Germany had indeed become a major threat.

Germany's rise in Europe was indeed a very recent fact. The Germans had barely had enough time to realize their new position on the international scene. Germany had just emerged the unlikely winner of a series of wars with major powers in Europe. It had been unified under the rule of Prussia after Prussia defeated rival German powers (1863-1866), Austria-Hungary (1866) and France (1870-1871). Prussia had developed over centuries a very efficient army. It was used to facing more powerful adversaries and planning ahead its next wars, compensating with greater tactical and technical skills for its numerical inferiority. By the late 1890s, Germany had decisively outstripped Austria-Hungary, which it had turned into a junior ally, France, whose army and economy were declining, and Russia, whose forces were lagging behind the standards of other European armies.[1] But German leaders had not fallen into a state of complacency. Instead, they lived to emulate their predecessors who had always prepared the next war.

Britain was an unlikely foe for Germany. Germany was a land power, while Britain was a sea power. Britain had no commitment on the continent and no significant army to attack Germany. Both nations had often been allies in the past and had come to consider that they shared more with one another than with any other nation. Both were Germanic people, Protestant nations, major industrial powers, advanced cultures. And their ruling families were closely related. The British Queen, Victoria, was actually the grandmother of the new German Emperor, Wilhelm. But Wilhelm was an ambitious young man who wanted to surpass Germany's founding father, his own mentor, the recently retired Bismarck. Bismarck had turned a loose confederation of weak to medium powers into the strongman of Europe. He had masterminded the foundation of a new German Empire and had installed it at the center of a network of alliances that all but guaranteed Germany against any significant threat. To surpass Bismarck, Wilhelm had recklessly elected to turn Germany from the European superpower it was, into the world superpower. Fulfilling that ambition meant, in Wilhelm's worldview, supplanting the actual world superpower, Britain.

Wilhelm presented a confrontation with Britain though it was inevitable. He reasoned that the rapidly growing economy of Germany demanded the command of overseas markets that could absorb its exports. A vast colonial empire was becoming necessary to sustain German expansion, and colonies, in turn, required a command of the seas. Germany could not afford to be cut off from its vital basis by the Royal Navy. The contrarian point of view was discarded. Germany, with the fastest-growing population and economy of all major European powers,[2] was not obviously hampered by the absence of its own large colonial empire. But this fact was increasingly considered as drag on German dynamism nonetheless, if only because

German industry was to some extent dependent on British and French colonial products, which could be cut off in case of war. In the 1870s and 1880s the British certainly viewed the French and the Russian navies as the major threats at sea. They had been keen to train the nascent German navy. These circumstances were discarded and, rather than to seek a close alliance with the British against any other colonial powers, from which a large empire could have been captured, the Germans elected in 1899 to build a High Seas Fleet that would be specifically and explicitly designed to attack the British Royal Navy.[3]

From 1899 on, Germany indeed committed a rapidly growing line of credit to that plan. Wilhelm was the supreme authority on defense and foreign policy. The heir of a successful regime, he commanded the loyalty of a vast majority in Parliament. His decision was not challenged. Its consequences were, however, decisive. From 1899, Germany turned itself into Britain's main foe. The bipolarization immediately resulted in policy convergence and the escalation of the means committed to war. For Britain, as with Germany, meeting the new threat implied a radical departure from previous strategies.

If Germany aimed at acquiring an instrument of power similar to Britain's, a first-class high-sea navy, the British reacted by aiming for instruments similar to Germany's. International alliances had hitherto been a distinctive German asset. Until 1890, German treaties with Russia, Austria-Hungary and Italy completely isolated France and Britain and made Germany the hub of continental alliances. In reaction, the British government put an end to its "splendid isolation." It signed a formal treaty of alliance with Japan in 1902. It also settled possible points of friction with German's adversaries in Europe: agreements, both formal and informal, were reached with France and Russia.[4] The British convergence with

Germany could also be observed in the reorganization of the army after 1900. It was transformed with a view to use it much more effectively abroad, against modern European armies. Last but not least, Britain converged with Germany regarding the management of the navy. From 1899, Germany had begun an unprecedented ten-year building program to develop a High Seas Fleet capable of challenging British supremacy. Admiral Tirpitz, the leading German High Seas Fleet designer, considered that while the German navy could not be expected to be of the same size as the British navy, the Germans could threaten the defense of the whole British Empire by concentrating their fleet in the North Sea, near the British coasts, thus forcing the British squadrons to abandon their positions all around the world to regroup in defense of the homeland. The British indeed reacted by concentrating their navy in the North Sea. And the officers most willing to make their crews battle-ready were promoted much more systematically than before by the Admiralty.[5]

But the British reaction could not limit itself to compensating for actual German assets. It was also meant to anticipate possible German moves and to prevent further surprises. The risk, it was felt, was to underestimate the threat. In consequence, Britain accelerated shipbuilding, and in 1905, Admiral John Fisher was made in charge of redesigning entirely the Royal Navy. He immediately decided to innovate in order to increase British firepower and decisively outgun the Germans. Learning from the only recent major battle between modern navies (the battle of Tsushima between the Russian and the Japanese fleets), Fisher deduced that long-range "big" guns were decisive in battle. They also had to be fitted on heavily armored hulls. A new type of ship emerged from these considerations, the all big-gun, one-purpose battleship, designed only to hunt and destroy other battleships. These

"Dreadnought-class" ships, like the first-class men-of-war of the Nelson era, could only serve to face an adversary who had resolved to pursue similar tactics. And indeed these innovations met with unexpected success: upon learning about the new class of British warships, Tirpitz ordered the German building program suspended for over a year, and in turn redesigned his own battleships and raised them to a standard comparable to the British.[6]

Ships and instruments were increasingly compared and improved in reaction to the other side's move. Between 1905 and 1914 both sides not only accelerated the production of battleships, but engaged both in the production of Dreadnought-class battleships, and then of ever larger Dreadnoughts, equipped with ever larger guns, more powerful engines, more streamlined internal layouts. That escalation also meant that the fleets converged on the same standards and the new units produced became increasingly comparable. It thus suddenly appeared that one side was actually outcompeting the other. The race to build more and better Dreadnoughts was clearly won by the British by 1912-1914. At that point it became evident that any major conflict involving both countries would have to be decided on land.[7] World War I was ready to unfold.

The run-up to World War I is a case study in bipolarization. The conflict erupted when both sides suddenly understood they had completely underestimated the threat posed by the other side. The bipolar escalation and convergence was typical. Each side designed countermeasures to check the advance of the other side and launched initiatives to check the next moves of the adversary.

This bipolarization was fueled by powerful personal feuds, first and foremost the rivalry that existed between the sovereigns of both nations. They inspired and encouraged the decisive moves on both sides. All diverging policies and alliances were discouraged. Only those that were vindicated by the reactions of the other side were continued.

Personal rivalries are always the fruit of frustrated alliances. Wilhelm II, the German Emperor, who more than anyone else initiated the arms race and created the conditions of a future world war, nourished a deep personal resentment. On the one hand, Wilhelm was closely related to the British Royal Family. He was the first grandchild of Queen Victoria to access a throne. He was also a fluent English speaker. Extremely attracted to some aspects of Britain, notably its navy, he was delighted to be made, among others, a British Admiral.[8] But on the other hand, he was not British. Moreover he insisted on ruling personally German foreign and military affairs. While this conformed to Prussian ways it was completely at odds with the British ones. In Britain the monarch was to serve the policy of an elected Parliament.[9] Wilhelm ignored this and sought to use his private correspondence with Queen Victoria and King Edward VII to bypass elected officials and push his own agenda, as if Victoria and her son were the autocrats he fancied himself. He naturally irritated them mightily. Their cold answers and their treatment of him as a foreigner in all official correspondence, in return frustrated Wilhelm immensely.

In fact, Wilhelm felt he did not receive the appreciation he deserved from the only peers he recognized, his British relatives.[10] He reacted by using every opportunity to act in a vexatious manner. He was particularly jealous of his Uncle Bertie, King Edward VII, who in turn disliked him intensely. This rivalry found a first outlet in yachting races. Both monarchs raced against one another in 1905, not far from the formidable British warships stationed at Cowes.[11]   It was therefore no accident that Wilhelm himself ultimately justified his foreign policy by explaining he wanted "ships of [his] own."[12] For him, the German policy was first and foremost the continuation of a bitter rivalry with the British sovereign.

Another deeply ambivalent anglophile was Alfred von Tirpitz whom Wilhelm II named to implement his naval agenda. On the one hand, Tirpitz sent his children to British schools and proclaimed his admiration for British culture.[13] He imitated Nelson by calling his aides his "band of brothers."[14] On the other hand, he never found in the British officers the recognition of peers and resented it.[15] He was the one who eventually obtained from the German Parliament the vote of funds for an unprecedented naval buildup – by designating for the first time in German history Britain as the main foe. His clear sense of purpose played an immense role in mobilizing the German Parliament. He masterminded the design of a High Seas Fleet composed mainly of battleships with the sole purpose of attacking and destroying the British Fleet, in opposition to his predecessors and rivals who had argued for lighter units designed to protected German trade lines all over the world. Tirpitz was constantly promoted and protected by Wilhelm II.

Once Wilhelm II had in effect launched an international bipolarization, all policies that were aligned with it were facilitated and all initiatives that were not aligned lost traction. There were influential British ministers in both parties, Liberal and Unionist, who promoted an alliance with Germany. But they never found powerful allies in Germany itself, and they eventually lost all influence.[16] By contrast, French ambassadors and ministers who sought overtures with the British government were actively coached by King Edward VII.[17]

The German naval policy generated huge tensions within the Royal Navy as two groups of British naval officers competed to impose a strategic response. In the end, the group that had best anticipated German moves was favored by the British government. The tensions within the navy had themselves all the characteristics of a fully mature bipolarization, but one which was deeply at odds with the international bipolarization. As a result, it did not find a deep echo in other sections of the British society. It had to end. The need to face the Enemy of the nation prevailed.

From 1900 to 1914 a group of Royal Navy officers designed radical reforms, while the other opposed them fiercely. The conflict was deeply political as well as technical. The first group intended to open up the ranks of the officers to worthy sailors of the lower classes, a distinctively equalitarian agenda, while the other group intensely resented that policy, which it labeled a breach of tradition. The first one was headed by Admiral John Fisher, the second by another Admiral, Lord Charles Beresford. Fisher was born far from England, in Ceylon, in a middle-class family. Beresford was the head of a wealthy noble family and cultivated the traditional lifestyle of the land-based aristocrat, hunting and riding horses in his Irish estate.[18] Fisher was ferociously determined to sap the domination of an upper-class conservative hierarchy within the Navy, which he named the "mandarins" and, more generally, the "Dukes and Duchesses."[19] Beresford and his group despised Fisher, whom, with reference to his colonial origins, and a suggestion that Fisher was not a pure-blood British man, they nicknamed "the mulatto."[20] The Fisher-Beresford antagonism intensely polarized the Navy. Leading officers could not be both "Fisherites" and friends of Beresford.[21]

Both Fisher and Beresford recognized that Germany was now the Enemy. Both saw the new German High Seas Fleet as the main threat to Britain. But while Fisher advocated concentrating the British Royal Navy in the North Sea, directly facing the German fleet, Beresford claimed that this move would excessively weaken the British Royal Navy elsewhere and eventually shatter the fabric of the British Empire around the world. While Fisher designed a new type of ship, the Dreadnought, to concentrate firepower in case of a major battle against the German High Seas Fleet, Beresford maintained that priority had to be given to the protection of the British trade lines by lighter, faster ships, like cruisers. Beresford argued that Fisher's new type of ship condemned all previous battleships, in which the British had enjoyed an overwhelming superiority.[22]

Fisher was vindicated by the arms race. The reaction of the adversary showed that his options, not Beresford's, were the correct ones. Indeed, in Germany, a symmetric debate had opposed Chancellor Hollmann who, like Beresford, supported lighter units, unlike Admiral Tirpitz and Fisher, who argued for concentration and battleships. After nearly a decade of hesitations, Tirpitz prevailed with Emperor Wilhelm.[23]

The Navy bipolarization never found a deep echo in the Parliament, in spite of its resemblance to a bipolarization between the Unionists-Conservatives, defenders of traditional hierarchies, and the Liberals, whose agenda was markedly more equalitarian. Beresford unsuccessfully lobbied to replace Fisher. A popular figure and a member of the House of Commons for the Conservatives since the 1870s, he did not seem up to the job anymore in the 1900s.[24] Balfour, the Conservatives leader, never planned to replace Fisher, whom he had installed in the first place. The Conservatives actually campaigned for more Dreadnought-class battleships. The British government, Parliament, and citizens were chiefly concerned with the threat of a possible German invasion.

As a result, the polarization between Fisher and Beresford increasingly appeared like a purely personal feud. The Cabinet, preoccupied with a lack of communication within the Navy in case of war, decided to remove both men from their functions. It eventually replaced Fisher with his most trusted lieutenant before calling him back as First Navy Lord when war broke out.

The international bipolarization dictated the agenda, the priorities and the incumbents. Not only the personal rivalries, but also the polarization in the British Parliament, were ultimately constrained by the more gripping international polarization that culminated with World War I. When policies were at odds with the international polarization, they were eventually forsaken, for all the passions that they may have provoked in the first place. For instance, the building of new battleships was given the priority upon the social programs in 1909-1910, at the apex of party polarization, although the Liberal government had made the social programs the cornerstone of its platform against the Conservatives. Eventually, both parties concurred in accepting war against Germany in August 1914.[25]

Personal rivalries and political opposition either aligned with the international bipolarization or had to yield to it. The most influential rivals, the two sovereigns, initiated the polarization that all others had to join. Their personal rivalry turned into a general bipolarization.

14. Beyond Reason
and Above All Laws

The mind imagines that a single malevolent will, the Enemy, is the cause of all evil. It foresees that his destruction will restore peace and bring back a golden age. The Enemy is understood to be the anomaly and the world is imagined as in a natural and perennial order, only temporarily disturbed by the misdeeds of the Enemy.

People and nations are therefore thought to be naturally reasonable and peaceful. Freed from the Enemy, they should rule themselves harmoniously and agree with each other about the common good.

But for the time being, acting reasonably simply cannot be enough to defeat the anomaly that is the Enemy. Since he has been able to disrupt the world's normal order, to counter his moves, to redress the wrongs he caused, requires some extraordinary measures.

Only the ones who share the same vision of the Enemy are not perturbed. They see their actions as rightful because they are exceptional, proportional to the evil that is fought and necessary to restore the normal state of the world. But these countermeasures are found to be deeply unreasonable by those who do not share the precise idea of the Enemy that justifies them.

As a result, any action is doomed to both attract some people and repulse others, producing hostility as well as support. The universal belief in natural reason does not make people more reasonable. It only makes them outraged at others not behaving reasonably.

Reason is imagined to be natural to humans, but it is thought it will only be observed once the present madness is over, when the Enemy is vanquished. Belief in reason is therefore particularly expressed during intense conflicts, when victory seems at hand, when it seems it will forever bring an end to evil. The end of wars, civil or international, is therefore strongly correlated with the foundation of new institutions designed to enable a government through reason.

These new institutions based on reason can be recognized by specific goals and means. They aim to restore natural rights that have been alienated. They aim to establish peace forever. They seek to avoid secrecy and promote open debates together with a large participation in decision-making.

For example, during the two world wars, the soon-to-be victorious powers designed institutions that reflected this vision. It inspired the creation of the League of Nations in 1920The drafters imagined institutions designed to be ruled by reason and therefore opposed to the secret and devious ways typically attributed to the Enemy. They sought, for example, to forbid secret treaties. This point had notably been emphasized in the first of *Fourteen Points* published by of the President of the United States, Woodrow Wilson, on January 8, 1918. Open diplomacy was to become the norm. Woodrow Wilson's Point 14 offered that it should be in the future processed through "a general association of nations."

In 1945, after World War II, the Charter of the United Nations Organization begins with the typical considerations:

> We the peoples of the United Nations determined:
>
> –to save succeeding generations from the scourge of war, which twice in our lifetime has brought untold sorrow to mankind, and
>
> –to reaffirm faith in fundamental human rights, in the dignity and worth of the human person, in the equal rights of men and women and of nations large and small, and
>
> –to establish conditions under which justice and respect for the obligations arising from treaties and other sources of international law can be maintained...[1]

Belief in reason is further illustrated by the design of deliberative assemblies meant to settle conflicts by open discussion. In order to facilitate expression of different points of view and a settlement, it is generally assumed that the more people concerned by the rule or by the decision, the larger the deliberating body should be. The largest body is always meant to enact the most general rules. This principle is found in all sorts of governing bodies, from the General Assembly of the United Nations to the assembly of the shareholders in a company, from the congress of a federal government like the United States to town councils, from the ancient Athenian Ecclesia to the contemporary National Congress of the Communist Party of China... Constitutions generally reserve the making of the most general regulations, the laws, to the largest assemblies that they provide. Legislative bodies are made of the whole people, the largest possible deliberative body, or are elected by the people. In consequence, when the executive is also elected by the whole people it tends to participate in the legislative process. Of course, in that case the "executive" is not purely an executioner of the legislator's commands, in spite of its name. For example, the President of the United States, indirectly elected by the people, can veto a bill, thus participating in the making of legislation (Article I, Section 7, Clause 2 of the Constitution).[2]

The notion that the common opinion is the best foundation for the law is also translated into words that associate both ideas, as in the Greek "doxa," which means both the common opinion and the law, or in the English "normal" that evokes the norm both in its legal and statistical meanings: what is considered to be the common law – the norm – and what is proper to all or at least to the vast majority of people.

The most intense conflicts generate the idea that they must be the last ones. But it shall never be so. A cycle of bipolarization is followed by another one. Once peace is declared, the seeds of other conflicts soon appear. And therefore, the beautiful institutions that were supposed to make peace last forever must soon seem perverted by secret cabals, lobbies, special and partisan interests, etc. No institution lasts forever; all are constantly up for reform.

For example, the institutions governing the United States were designed during the War of Independence (1775-1783). Soon their adoption, and their very vitality, produced unintended consequences which were interpreted as deep flaws. Competition for positions of power generated a bipartisan alignment and also diverging conceptions about the social fabric. Partisanship gradually aligned with these opposed views. In time this bipolarization generated another conflict, the Civil War (1861-1865).

Although they were meant to settle once and for all conflicts within the United States, the 1776 Declaration of Independence and the 1787 Constitution contained the points that would cleave the country apart a few decades later.

An early example that illustrates this is the decision of the Supreme Court of the United States in the landmark case *Marbury v. Madison* (1803). The Court ruled that a federal law could not contradict the Constitution and that the courts could decide not to uphold a law they found unconstitutional. This rule was not written in the Constitution but has ever since been presented by the Supreme Court as a necessary consequence of the text.[3] Yet, the decision was immediately contested by the President of the United States, Thomas Jefferson. He refused that the legislative power be subjected to the judiciary. Jefferson was a member of the Democratic-Republican Party, contrary to Chief Justice Marshall, who was a Federalist.

Even the simplest constitution is a source of bipolar conflicts. They stem out of the unforeseen but also from the paradoxes they contain, even in their most fundamental provisions.

For example, the Constitution of the United States, adopted on June 21, 1788, starts with the words, "We the People of the United States of America." It means that the People of the United States are the authors of the Constitution. Yet the Constitution also creates the United States of America. As a result, the People of the USA are both the author and the product of the Constitution.

A similar paradox can be found in the first words of the Declaration of Independence adopted on July 4, 1776: "We hold these truths to be self-evident, that all men are created equal...." Not only was it necessary to state these truths and write them down in a most solemn form but, as the Declaration itself recognizes, they were ignored in spite of their proclaimed self-evidence. Both paradoxes were in the following decades at the core of radically opposed interpretations.

In the wake of the American Civil War, the right of the People to secede from the Union they had adopted, to undo what they had done, was proclaimed by supporters of the Southern secessionist states, while those who opposed them held that the Constitution of the United States had not provided a right to secede from it. A key argument in the debates was whether the People were the product of the Constitution or its creator.

Likewise, the self-evident equality of "men" proclaimed by the Declaration of Independence was much tested as both sides fought over the right of blacks to be included among the "men" considered equals by the Declaration. This interpretation was proclaimed to be self-evident by the Union's President-elect Abraham Lincoln, in Philadelphia on February 22, 1861, as Lincoln travelled towards Washington were he would soon assume the Presidency of the United States. But his interpretation was far from self-evident for his most determined adversaries, who at the exact same time had begun to secede from the Union.[4]

Each time, the problem must seem specific. But the real cause behind the impossibility of obtaining a general agreement to an action is that an action is always meant to be a reaction, a way to redress something that went wrong by an equivalent and contrary move. It is justified as a rightful revenge against an abnormal disruption of the world order. However, it appears paradoxical, abnormal and revolting to all those who do not share in the same idea of the Enemy. The actions are justified by the desire to bring peace, but they regularly provoke outrage.

For example, the Peace Treaties that created the League of Nations also considered that many territories claimed by

Germany and Austria-Hungary had to be allocated to different nations. The treaties were thus resented by the vanquished as the creation of artificial states rather than the restoration of free nations. They were seen as a "Diktat," not as a reasonable contract between sovereign nations. They provided a cause for seeking revenge.

In the eyes of the promoters of a measure, the action is always justified: it is conceived as a mere proportional reaction, a necessity to redress an evil situation. For example, in June 1940 Adolf Hitler required that the armistice between Germany and France be signed in the very same train wagon and in the same place, Rethondes, where both countries had signed the armistice in 1918. He thus signified that the German victory erased its unjust defeat in 1918. According to him, it was a justified reaction against the abnormal treatment of Germany at the hands of the victors in 1918. Significantly, Hitler also had the car destroyed shortly before the ultimate German defeat in 1945, meaning that he would never accept it.

In these examples we can observe the origins of the legal principle of parallelism of forms. An act that nullifies or replaces a previous act must be adopted in the same way as the original one. It seems a mere technicality, a routine legal principle. Yet parallelism of form finds its direct origin in the notion of rightful reaction.

Any action is justified by those who advocate it as a reaction. However, it is bound to create disbelief and resentment among those who do not share the exact same understanding of who the Enemy is. For anyone who does not share it, although the action claims the existence of a natural, stable order, it paradoxically aims to deliberately destroy it.

An example of such opposition in arguments can be observed in Welsh-language schooling. It shows how people can react in opposed ways to a policy. Schooling children in Welsh in Wales may well appear at first glance quite normal and natural. But English is the most used language in Welsh schools. It is also the main language used every day by most of the people living in Wales. This is precisely what the promoters of a Welsh-language education aim to change. But by acting so, they are also at risk of appearing to disrupt a situation others deem normal.[5]

The perception of a deliberate disruption may be reinforced by a series of specific measures. First, the language taught in Welsh-language schools is deliberately different from the sort of Welsh that can be heard spoken outside of schools. Many new words have been created. They are meant to be learned by pupils and to replace on the long-term words which are currently used by Welsh people. Dr. Jones, a prominent Welsh-language activist, explained to me how Breton, another Celtic language, is used as a source of inspiration to coin new Welsh words. Even in the Welsh-speaking heartland, in North-Western Wales, where schools are officially labeled "naturally Welsh-speaking schools," promoters of Welsh-speaking education usually prefer to establish special Welsh-language schools like the ones that exist in other parts of Wales. They do not actually seek to use the "natural" language in the only place where it could have been preserved. Finally, Welsh-language schools are promoted as schools that obtain better-than-average results, suggesting that their ultimate goal may not be to promote Welsh but rather to create elite schools.[6]

Activists do not see their action as the creation of an artificial and paradoxical situation, though. They consider that these measures are simply legitimate to compensate for the effects of the English conquest. They believe them necessary to restore a national continuity that has been destroyed. Contrary to many other Welsh people, they do not see the present linguistic situation in Wales as the result of a process of natural degenerescence of Welsh and its replacement by a more dynamic language, English, but as the abnormal result of a foreign aggression that started in the Middle-Ages and lasted to this day. They feel that Welsh is highly contaminated with English syntax and vocabulary, even in the Welsh heartland. The language must be expurgated of words of English origin. Simply recruiting "naturally Welsh-speaking" children would not be enough to make pupils feel comfortable with the Welsh language; they would be tempted to switch to English, especially if the sort of Welsh they speak, peppered as it is with English words, seems to them some English dialect. Finally, to enhance pride in the language implies making pupils proud of joining top schools.[7] Thus they do not see any paradox in their policies.

The activists' arguments simply cannot be understood and approved if one does not share the idea that the Welsh national history has been disrupted by an English invasion so that a self-supporting, perennial community needs to be actively re-created as it had been actively destroyed by the Enemy. Welsh activists have illustrated their desire to reverse history and to liberate Wales from England in a collage, entitled *The Dragon's Revenge*. It shows a red dragon overcoming a knight. The knight lies on the ground, with the dragon's claws on his chest. The red dragon is the symbol of Wales. The knight is Saint George, the symbol of England. In the usual version of the legend, Saint George kills the dragon. By inverting positions, and putting the dragon on top of a defeated Saint George, the authors expressed their desire to rightfully reverse history and to lead a Welsh rising against English aggression (*Figure 14* and *Figure 15*).

Figure 14. The Dragon's Revenge *(1990).*[8]

The dragon, symbol of Wales, defeats Saint George, the symbol of England.

Figure 15. The original story (1515).[9]

Saint George, patron of England, kills the dragon.

In Wales as elsewhere, the historic disruption is always seen as exceptional and abnormal. It is always thought that elsewhere things are less conflictual, more conforming to the natural order. For instance, Welsh-language activists would not compare the situation of their language with that of English in the United States or of French in France, which they do not deem to be endangered languages. They see their situation as abnormal. However, in the last decades activists that have actually sought to protect English in the US against the invasion of Spanish, notably by fostering a "national" language status for English. Likewise, French was recognized in France as the "language of the Republic" in order to limit the promotion of "regional" languages like Basque or Breton and the penetration of English.[10]

*

The mind constantly produces paradoxes. It cannot imagine order without imagining at the same time its disruption, anomalies; to redress these anomalies seems to necessitate further extraordinary measures. But it is also this paradoxical logic which sets our world in motion and which, ultimately, creates it.

People do not act out of reason. They do not follow a stable course, nor do they mean to. They aim to react to an abnormal situation. They believe they can set a course back to the golden age but they really produce constant change. There is no lasting peace, no stable community in a world driven by the quest for heroism.

However, most theories have explained human affairs by assuming the existence of coherent and stable wholes. They were imagined as systems, composed of elements which interacted harmoniously, performing stable functions or else adjusted to maintaining the stable whole. The problem was that systems could not account for the permanent conflicts and dynamics of the real world. To a large degree this paradigm of stability is still very much in use, largely for lack of a coherent alternative, as observations in all domains clearly do not confirm its premises.

First of all systems cannot explain their own origins and transformations. In a constantly changing world, this entails serious shortcomings, even for the most ambitious theories. For example, Ernest Gellner developed one of the most systematic explanations of the industrial revolution and of modern nationalism. According to him, they could only exist in association with one another. He assumed that a large industry required a mobile workforce with a standard education and culture, while modern nationalism would favor the abolition of internal barriers and a state-standardized schooling system.[11] In short, modern nationalism would make the industrial revolution possible and vice-versa, which would explain their simultaneous emergence in Western Europe.

Gellner explained why industrialization and nationalization could only exist in conjunction with one another. And therefore he could not explain how such a system first emerged. Gellner pointed out that such societies had not always existed. He distinguished modern industrial societies from pre-modern agrarian ones. He described how the pre-modern state would, contrary to the modern one, maintain local communities in relative isolation. Only the elites could access a shared language and culture in an agrarian world.[12] Gellner ascribed to industrial societies a greater material power that enabled them to conquer the agrarian world and transform it.[13] But he could not explain how they first emerged from the agrarian world. This was bound to remain a "mystery."[14]

The next and certainly the most important difficulty in applying systemic explanations to human reality is of course the deep paradoxes that, as we just saw, can be found even in the most fundamental principles invoked to justify action.

Conflicts are inherent to human affairs, as is the will to end them. Law is a major product of conflict resolution. But law itself is not exempt from conflicts and such conflicts eventually result in conflicts of norms which must themselves be solved. Thus a "hierarchy of norms" was imagined with a view to make norms of higher rank prevail upon conflictual lesser norms. Different levels of norms can be distinguished: the law, both federal and state-level, general regulations, particular decisions, precedents, etc. They all rest on a fundamental text: all legal decisions, even the most particular ones, are supposed to be ultimately based on a "fundamental law," also called a "constitution." The other sources of law only have what authority is granted to them, directly or indirectly, by the constitution.[15] However, the constitution itself is a prominent source of conflict. There is no such thing as a legal system in human affairs.

Even the authors that are the most attached to emphasizing the state's legal foundations, must start from other premises to explain its real workings. For instance, Max Weber and contemporary authors like René Carré de Malberg[16] departed from a purely legal definition of the state. Weber underlined that: "a state is a human community that (successfully) claims the monopoly of the legitimate use of physical force within a given territory."[17] For Weber and, before him, Jean-Jacques Rousseau, "violence" is simply the opposite of lawful and legitimate action. It is not based on reason and ignores the general will of the members of the community.[18]

Generalizing the problem, Jean Leca argued that no legal argument or provision contains a coherent explanation of its own existence, either it is a code of laws, a constitution, a piece of international legislation, or even a fundamental human right.[19] He pointed out that all justifications are inherently paradoxical because humans invoke principles but fundamentally cultivate heroic dreams, and engage in partisanship and conflicts; they must bypass the principles they acknowledge.

Going yet further, we can observe that no system can explain human language. Like human "communities," "nations" or "states," "languages" are the objects of human endeavors, policies and conflicts. They change, not of their own accord, according to their own laws, but through the plans made for them, the measures taken by their promoters, and their successes or failures.

There is no neutral language, a pure medium of the thought, a way to convey information regardless of the commitments, alliances and conflicts of the people in presence. Each word, sentence and narrative carries an intent that is not limited to its explicit and immediate meaning but that implicitly deals with the defense of a community, of an order, and a special relationship between the people in presence that is both potentially an alliance and a conflagration.

Noam Chomsky was right to contradict Ferdinand de Saussure's and Roman Jakobson's proposal. Languages cannot be approached as systems. Chomsky indeed observed that people have an innate capacity to decipher new sentences, to learn and create new rules and languages.[20] He proposed to discover the principles of the universal "generative grammar" that allows them to do this.

We know now the logic that makes them capable of doing so. It rules the human mind and the human world. It applies to all actions and to all thoughts. It is a law that means change everywhere and always.

IV

A GENERAL MOBILIZATION

Each one secretly dreams of being a superior being, the Hero, detached from all bounds, first of all material ones. But one also feels one must achieve the highest possible material position as any policy necessarily entails the production and redistribution of assets.

Each one believes they are different because they are aware of the danger. They believe they are different from ordinary people, who are unaware, and therefore are simply egoistic, materialistic and greedy *(15 – Fighting Alongside Companions)*.

Ordinary people are easily manipulated by the Enemy. But companions believe they cannot simply evoke the Enemy with ordinary people; this would only scare them away. Companions agree they must first detach ordinary people from the Enemy and attract them to the cause by providing more goods and service than their adversaries *(16 – Enlisting Ordinary* People*)*.

As alliances solidify and conflicts intensify, each camp seeks to enlist more supporters by producing and redistributing more than the other side *(17 – Competing to Mobilize)*. Production and redistribution rise and decline with the conflict. All human activities are synchronized with the general bipolarization. They all obey the same, general dynamics *(18 – Producing and Distributing to Overcome)*.

15. Fighting Alongside Companions

Deep inside, without even realizing it, each one is driven to imagine they are a unique being, distinct from all other people, who appear by contrast all the more comparable to one another. They seem ordinary: they appear to follow a standard, a norm, which makes them replicable and exchangeable.

By association of ideas, each one imagines that ordinary people are primarily motivated by a desire for what can be reproduced, exchanged, especially the most standardized and tradable good, money. They would want to accumulate as much money and as many goods as possible. It is through their lust for goods and money that the Enemy would subvert the ordinary people who ignore his existence.

The companions, the people who share the knowledge of the Enemy's misdeeds among themselves, also share between themselves views on ordinary people: they distinguish each other from ordinary people and praise among themselves detachment from material desires and sacrifices willingly made.

These notions are perfectly illustrated by one of the most famous speeches, delivered by King Henry at the battle of Agincourt, in William Shakespeare's *Henry V* (1599); Act IV, Scene 3[1]:

If we are mark'd to die, we are enow
To do our country loss; and if to live,
The fewer men, the greater share of honour …
By Jove, I am not covetous for gold…
But if it be a sin to covet honour,
I am the most offending soul alive…
That he which hath no stomach to this fight,
Let him depart, his passport shall be made,
And crowns for convoy put into his purse:
We would not die in that man's company,
That fears his fellowship to die with us.
This day is call'd the feast of Crispian:
He that outlives this day, and comes safe home…

…he'll remember, with advantages
What feats he did that day. Then shall our names,
Familiar in his mouth as household words,
Harry the King, Bedford and Exeter,
Warwick and Talbot, Salisbury and Gloucester,
Be in their flowing cups freshly remember'd.
This story shall the good man teach his son;
And Crispin Crispian shall ne'er go by,
From this day to the ending of the world,
But we in it shall be remember'd.
We few, we happy few, we band of brothers;
For he to-day that sheds his blood with me,
Shall be my brother: be he ne'er so vile,
This day shall gentle his condition:

> And gentlemen in England, now a-bed,
> Shall think themselves accurs'd they were not here....

Shakespeare's play builds on historic events: the life of the real King Henry V evokes in many ways a heroic warrior. The king actually won the battle at Agincourt in 1415 with a small English army against vastly superior French knights. The victory secured him the throne of France which his adversaries had denied him. Peace between the two nations seemed certain until the king died an untimely death.

Shakespeare's play inspired generations of English fighters. Admiral Horatio Nelson quoted it frequently and tried to make his lieutenants and soldiers feel like the "band of brothers" evoked by Shakespeare.[2] Prime Minister Winston Churchill proclaimed on August 20, 1940, when British pilots alone faced the Nazi air force, "Never... was so much owed by so many to so few." This sentence was later heralded in a film, the *Battle of Britain.*[3] Both Nelson and Churchill, at the head of a small English army facing a vastly superior adversary, must have felt that they were the real English hero, the one in charge of facing the most dangerous threat, the one whose victory would decide the fate of their country and secure peace forever. The terms used by Shakespeare have been felt to render heroic attitude perfectly. He played with notions that are at the core of the heroic dream.

The personal reasons that led Henry V to make war are developed in earlier parts of the play: Henry's rightful outrage at being denied the French Crown, his being forced into the conflict. The speech before the battle is the apex of the play. It evokes feelings that can touch anyone.

Henry's speech evokes a battle that will decide the fate of his country for all eternity, "to the ending of the world," a battle that will be remembered forever, and whose victors will be praised and indeed worshiped by all. Henry proves himself up to his heroic vision: he is ready to sacrifice everything he possesses, even his own life. He scorns nothing more than the egoistic, greedy people that preferred to stay "in their beds," comfortably away from the fight, or those that followed him with a view to make a fortune out of the spoils of war. Even if defeat is highly likely in the face of a formidable foe, the king is happy to get rid of them. He even offers them a last incentive to leave.

Henry wants on the contrary, no distinctions to be made between him and any of his companions, the brothers at arms that would stay with him at all costs. Although he is king, the first in his country, he admits that the battle to come, because it is to be decisive, is the only real source of distinction. The fellowship that unites him with his companions is in his eyes the most important thing in the world. The whole idea holds onto one line: "We few, we happy few, we little band of brothers." The radical distinction between the ordinary selfish materialistic person and the heroic fighter and their companions is an integral part of the heroic dream.

Shakespeare re-enacts history to make Henry's speech depict in vibrant terms a dream to which one is irresistibly attracted. It may be that Henry's speech would not be the most effective in a real encounter. To make soldiers leave on the eve of battle may discourage others. But Shakespeare wrote his play for the merchants of London. Accumulating "gold" was indeed their chief activity. They indeed paid to watch the play. And yet, Shakespeare produced for them the most inspirational hero, a man who was remembered as the perfect king by his people and who did not distinguish himself by accumulating gold but by facing, with only his companions, the most formidable danger. The success of the play testifies that it touched a very sensitive chord indeed.

The notion of ordinary people only makes sense by opposition to the Hero and his companions. Otherwise it is not a coherent idea. Ordinary people are imagined both as inferior and as average. This is illustrated by the two, apparently disconnected, if not contradictory meanings of the word "mean," which applies to people and objects alike. It implies "low quality," "of poor, shabby, inferior quality or status," "worthy of little regard: contemptible," "lacking dignity or honor: base" and "lacking in mental discrimination: dull." But it also means, in marked contrast, "of intermediary quality." The concept of an average, of an arithmetic "mean" is derived from this second meaning.[4] Both meanings are in fact derived from the same notion of ordinary, comparable people and objects. The first reflects the opposition between ordinary and special. In that sense, being ordinary is like being inferior. The second meaning reflects the comparability of ordinary items, which allows reducing them to a single value, the mean.

*

No one ever thinks of themselves as an ordinary person. Instead, people always distinguish themselves from ordinary people. This can for instance, be observed in scientific research. Theories describe and explain norms of behaviors. They inevitably suggest the people to whom they apply are ordinary. As a result, scientists, who do not see themselves as ordinary of course, tend to imagine more easily theories that apply to groups to which they believe they do not belong. For example, philologists detected a common structure in fairy tales, which were supposedly passed by maids or wives to children. They imagined that these tales came from ancient myths which were assumed to be the product of primitive, irrational and rural people. They recognized similarities with myths produced by exotic people. But they never discovered a similar structure in historical accounts. For centuries, philologists easily produced theories to explain other groups than their own. But they never applied these theories to themselves, self-styled civilized, rational, urban men. They saw, on the contrary, their own "History" as a unique chain of events that could not be judged by any other standard.

Since everyone desires to be distinguished from ordinary materialistic, egoistic people, no notion has been as widely applied in describing human affairs than the idea that people are chiefly attracted by the selfish accumulation of tradable goods. It is presently known as the "rational choice" theory.

It is difficult avoiding it. So we have no choice but to analyze it. The first problem is that it is notoriously difficult to explain what interest purely egoistic people have in coordinating their actions with other people.

Mancur Olson thought he had discovered a case that would help solve the problem. According to Olson, it was possible to use the rational choice theory to explain why a labor union would try to secure advantages for its members only. Olson considered this policy to be necessary for the union's survival, because if any employee could benefit from the advantages gained by the union, no one would want to adhere to the union. All would simply "free ride," benefiting from the union's efforts and money while investing nothing into it.[5] It is transparent that Olson reproduced closely the views of the union's leaders. They considered themselves a small minority of selfless activists and distinguished themselves from ordinary people, who they saw as consumed by egoistic desires for tradable goods, people who had to be coerced into collective action.

In fact, contrary to his intentions, Olson gave us the key as to why selfish materialism can never be turned into a general explanation: if everyone were egoistic, all would free ride, no one would have created the union or the company in the first place. They would have waited for others to do so. There would have been no "institution" to incite or force free-riders to act collectively in spite of their natural inclinations.

Rational choice theorists are thus typically led to explain collective ("macro") and individual ("micro") actions separately.[6] They tend to avoid facing what Kuklinski has called "problems of aggregation": they cannot explain how "the macro polity shapes individual beliefs and behavior, which in turn influence the larger collective, which in turn conditions the individual thinking and behavior, and so on."[7]

In a world populated by purely selfish people, there would be no coalitions and no collective conflicts either. Thomas Schelling correctly claimed that rational materialistic people would be "deterred" from engaging in major conflicts because "there is a powerful common interest in reaching an outcome that is not enormously destructive in values to both sides."[8] Likewise, Paul Sabatier pointed out that "if the opponent is evil, then its victory is likely to result in very substantial costs."[9]

However, egoistic, rational materialistic people would simply free-ride and start absolutely no conflict at all. They would wait for someone else to fight and sacrifice themselves in their stead. Sabatier inferred correctly that some "devil shift" must prevail over rational choice.

However, it would probably be simpler to point out that no one would live in a society guided by "rational choice." Selfish materialists simply cannot cooperate. They cannot have an interest in the well-being of others, let alone for a desire to sacrifice themselves for the common good.[10]

Interestingly, there is a second problem with "rational choice" that leads to a similar conclusion.

The rational choice theory supposes that not all desires can be fulfilled at the same time, because of the general "scarcity" of goods, the cause of which remains unclear. The point is that people must make rational choices in "trade-offs between meeting one desire and meeting another." The mind must necessarily choose to leave some desires unfulfilled. It is supposed to operate this choice according to the maximal satisfaction of its desires, the "maximization of utility."[11]

But if this was really its supreme goal and if the mind was able out of necessity to ignore or repress desires, then the logical result would be that it would repress all its desires, because this would be the most straightforward way to maximize satisfaction: no displeasure would be felt, all desires would be fulfilled even if, at the same time, no other desire would be fulfilled than the supreme one.

Such a result would of course be incompatible with any form of life. However, a less coherent, and perhaps less radical line of reasoning has inspired multiple philosophical or religious schools from antiquity: Stoics, Epicureans and various forms of monachism or asceticism have advocated, as a way to reach a superior state of happiness, some form of renouncement of the desires that could lead to frustration. They have particularly praised a detachment from desires which depend on material contingencies.

Compared to the two first problems, the third one may justly appear of lesser importance. It deserves its share of attention nonetheless due to the popularity of the notions that underlie it in many academic circles.

In order not only to "maximize," but also to merely increase one's satisfaction, one should pay considerable attention to the actions of other people who could influence the outcome of one's calculations.[12] As a result, it would be "rational" to try and forecast them and, assuming that other people are equally "rational," to render one's own actions predictable in order to influence them to do the same. Actions should become increasingly stable.[13] However, such tendency towards equilibrium is not to be found in human affairs.

The egoistic, materialistic individual known as "homo economicus" is a scientific dead-end. But it endures because it is based on notions that are rooted in the very structure of the mind.

16. Enlisting Ordinary People

Companions distinguish themselves from ordinary people. Companions extol sacrifices made to the common cause, while ordinary people seem selfish and materialistic, unaware of the threats that lie upon them. Companions naturally imagine that it is the ordinary people's greed for wealth that enables the Enemy to lure them.

And so companions are wary of disclosing their real purposes in the presence of ordinary people. This would scare them away. It would seem to put their material welfare at risk. Companions practice doublespeak.

As a result, in spite of their emphasis on sacrifice, companions have paradoxically a shared interest in producing and accumulating wealth to enlist ordinary people. Each one conceives of one's actions as noble even though they are but a means to achieve higher ends.

These beliefs cannot be shaken. Even when ordinary people reveal themselves to be less selfish than presumed, it merely confirms to companions that they have successfully detached someone from the Enemy's nets.

The belief that ordinary people are selfish and materialistic cannot be shaken. It was one of the early problems I faced during my research. I remember recognizing it one evening as an officer of the Irish Language Board invited me to observe an "information meeting" near Dublin. In the Republic of Ireland most children are schooled through English, but anyone can ask for an Irish-language education. The ministry of education must grant parents the type of schooling they choose for their children, provided competent teachers can be found and a schooling ground provided. The Irish Language Board facilitates such demands by gathering personnel, resources and also by encouraging parents to make the choice of an Irish-language education. This was the purpose of the "information meeting" for parents I observed.

On the way to our destination, the Irish Language Board officer explained to me that a group of parents had established a local committee and would lead the meeting. The Board would only be there to help with material and expert information. The line of argument would be that Irish-language education makes children bilingual. Bilingualism makes them more intelligent and successful in life. It was all about reassuring parents and convincing them they would make the best choice for their children. There must be no allusions to the history of Ireland or language conflicts. This would scare parents away.

Everything seemed to happen as planned until one member of the assembly rose and delivered, in a highly emotional tone, a speech arguing in substance that learning Irish was not a choice for Irish people. It was their heritage. Claiming it back was their duty. The "revolution" was not yet over, he concluded. Almost all rose in support and applauded enthusiastically. On the way back, the Board officer seemed genuinely satisfied. Parents were reassured. It all went according to plan. Bilingualism had convinced them.[1]

I seemed to be the only one that noticed that "parents" did not exactly behave as expected. They did not shy away from politics, conflicts and history. Quite the contrary, actually.

Their choice might not have been dictated only by a desire to acquire bilingualism. This situation struck me as recurrent as I had already witnessed similar meetings in Alsace and Wales. I had thought the situations exceptional then. I suddenly realized they were not and I had to explain why the beliefs "language experts" entertained about parents were never shaken by contrarian experiences.

The same disjunction between beliefs and observations transpired from a study of the motivations of people enlisting in Irish-language schools. Two researchers, Riagáin and Gliasáin, had detected that at least some parents were behaving much more like "activists" than ordinary people. In order to better understand the impact of that surprising attitude on the future development of Irish-language schools, the researchers conducted a survey and interviews to measure the relative size and specific characteristics of both populations: activists and ordinary parents. It turned out that they could not distinguish them. Too many behaved both as parents and activists. This puzzled the researchers.[2] But it obviously did not shake the language experts' notion that in general, parents were mostly narrowly interested in the material welfare of their children, contrary to activists and language experts that would accept to sacrifice much to the cause.

This enduring belief was all the more surprising because it came at a price, not only in Ireland but also in other countries where similar schooling systems had been developed. Indeed, opponents did regularly point out that the schools were not really about restoring a genuine linguistic or national community, but merely about instituting an elite schooling system. It was difficult for activists to counter these arguments since they did not want to openly present their actions in a conflictual light. On the contrary, the desire to avoid as much as possible allusion to the conflict often made them produce excessive arguments in the other direction. For example, one leaflet distributed in Alsace to promote Alsatian-speaking (or German-speaking) schools incorporated the slogan: "make a classy choice." The cartoon showed a pupil in a uniform that would not have been out of context in Eton, but certainly did not reflect in any measure the reality of Alsatian schools.

The activists I observed certainly practiced doublespeak. But they were not hypocrites. They did not seek to deceive their audience nor did they tell them willful lies. Most of them had opted to sign their own children in the schools they promoted. Some had learned themselves the language they promoted. Some had joined linguistic circles when they had decided to enlist other parents to obtain the type of education they desired for their children. They rejoiced at their children receiving a quality education and were proud to belong to a community that they felt was better off than most others in the country. In short, they shared in the beliefs that they attributed to ordinary people.

However, they explained their motivations to each other in radically different terms. When confidently together with like-minded people, they admitted that they were making sacrifices because they felt they had no choice but to help keep their national and linguistic community alive. Activists frequently mentioned how they had personally been victims of intolerant and bullying practices at school, like they were wearing a shameful "symbol" for speaking their preferred language.

Only when the bipolarization becomes quite intense do activist feel they need not anymore conceal their experiences to ordinary people because everyone is then conscious of the Enemy. For example, Ernest Lavisse, narrator of a primary school textbook on the history of France (1913), wrote therein about his own suffering as a child when he was bombarded by

German artillery.[3] One year later France and Germany were at war again. The only time I witnessed activists testifying in public about their own misery was during a public meeting where they had been confronted by their adversaries[4]. Only in the presence of an evidently hostile party did they not drop the pretense of being only interested in elite education.

So activists practiced the two logics at the same time. They cared to distinguish them but they were obviously not separable. It turns out that people imagine two different ways of thinking and of living, and attribute these two ways to completely distinguish people. But in fact, everyone personally follows both logics.

The discovery of the universal quest for heroism at last allows us to understand why each one believes they are not ordinary, materialistic people and why they feel at the same time that they must produce, accumulate and redistribute goods and services nonetheless. They feel they must do it to distinguish themselves in the eyes of ordinary people and enlist them to their cause.

17. Competing to Mobilize

Ordinary, materialistic people seem so easily manipulated by the Enemy. To detach them from the Enemy and mobilize them against him, one cannot simply reveal to them the dangers they face. One must attach them to the cause by providing them with more wealth and a better status than the Enemy. Each side perceives a competition with the other. As bipolarization rises, equality is increasingly favored.

Britain experienced a marked rise of equalitarianism during World War II. A large majority of the population rapidly came to accept that wealth should be better redistributed in their country. Their avowed goal was to offset the seductions exercised by the Enemy and fully mobilize the British people to the defense of their country.

During the first years of the war, Britain's aggressors spearheaded by Germany, Italy and the Soviet Union, seemed to be on the winning side. In Britain it was widely perceived that the dictators of these countries, Hitler, Mussolini and Stalin, could find an echo in the British territories by denouncing the British democracy as the oppression of the people by a privileged ruling class, and the British colonial empire as the abnormal domination of many people by a single people. Sweeping measures were increasingly desired to counter their attacks.

The following article illustrates how the idea of increasing equality rapidly gained acceptance as a necessity to win the war. It was published in *The Times* on July 1, 1940, at a time when Britain seemed to stand alone against all its adversaries. More equality was not envisaged as a temporary expedient to satisfy an unruly people, but as a permanent transformation of the British society, one capable of offering an adequate answer to Soviet and Fascist programs, one that would mobilize sufficiently the British to repel the advancing armies and ultimately defeat them. The article claimed that Britain had to offer something different and better than that of the "enemy" in order to win. It called for "a new social and international order" based on more "equality" as the condition for a British victory.

> The new order cannot be based on the preservation of privilege whether the privilege be that of a country, or a class or of an individual.[1]

At the core of that reasoning was the notion that ordinary people are mobilized not exclusively by a sense of duty but also, if not primarily, by the material conditions that are offered to them. Illustrating this, a 1943 Ministry of Information Home Intelligence report selected the following quote by a lower-class man as an exemplar of the sheer desirability and urgency of equalitarian measures to mobilize the people:

> It will make the ordinary man think that the country at last has some regard for him as he is supposed to have regard for the country.[2]

It is likely that the quote drew particular attention as it was from an "ordinary man" using that exact expression. Note that the quote does not mention wealth redistribution but dignity. It is unclear how the author of the report understood it, as a quote of an ordinary man expressing in his own words a demand for more redistribution or as the demand of a fellow countryman, illegitimately downgraded as "an ordinary man," for dignity. Both are possible and both meanings can coexist of course as, once the necessity for more equality has been accepted, it becomes all the easier to consider other people, not as "ordinary" but as equals, as companions. This unintended shift explains why more equality remained a policy priority in Britain several years after World War II had been won.

The structural and spontaneous nature of the reasoning can be illustrated by the fact that all major parties seemed to share the same fundamental understanding. Winston Churchill, Prime Minister and leader of the Conservative Party, advocated only a somewhat slower and more limited redistribution than the other parties. Although he justified his position in a way typical of a Conservative ideologue, he ultimately relied on the same considerations as the other parties: a will to mobilize the British as effectively as possible. He indeed claimed he accepted a gradual increase in equality, not a radical one, in order not to prompt a revolution by creating "false hopes" and "anger." He was adamant that this more measured transfer was necessary for it to be credible and thus effective in mobilizing the British.[3]

Widespread support for more equality lasted throughout the war. It explains the particularly favorable reception of the "Beveridge Report" which distinguished itself by its singularly systematic application of equalitarian measures. The principles invoked was:

> Everyone pays the same amount in contributions to insure themselves against temporary (unemployment or illness) or permanent (invalidity, old age) loss of income; everyone receives the same benefit.[4]

Opinion polls showed that a huge majority of the population was in favor of the measures advocated by the report. Even among those who would not benefit from them, support prevailed: 75 percent of the "top income group" and 90 percent of the other workers who would not directly gain in revenue, according to a Gallup poll.[5]

The Beveridge Report enacted a convergence with the Enemy's policies. Indeed, it advocated direct management by the state of the different types of social insurance rather than one which would be, in large part, in the hands of unions and charities[6]. British Labour in particular had been a strong adversary of direct management by the state before the war because this type of policy had been perceived as being engineered by conservative governments to weaken unions and support for popular movements. It was associated with Bismarck and Hitler in Germany as well as with Mussolini in Italy. During the remaining years of the War, initial hostility to state management withered away. Building a British "welfare state" became an acceptable reaction to the German "warfare state." This unintended convergence was the result of the will to react to the Enemy's policies.

During war, people tend to imagine that victory will somehow mark the end of history and that the changes they introduce will last forever after. But once the Enemy has been vanquished, people tend to regard again the desire of other people for wealth as greed and materialism. Support for more equality declines over time.

This reverse tendency is illustrated by interviews conducted with Vaclav Havel and Adam Michnik. Both Havel and Michnik considered themselves, and were generally recognized in their respective countries, Czech Republic and Poland, as leaders in the movement that prompted the fall of the Communist regimes in 1989-1990. Vaclav Havel was later elected and re-elected President of the Republic. Adam Michnik became the editor-in-chief of the *Gazeta Wyborcza*, an influential Polish daily newspaper.

Havel and Michnik recognized each other as companions: people who shared a common Enemy, and who underwent similar sufferings. Havel and Michnik recognized that they were both among the very few to resist the Communist regime.[7] At the time, twenty years before the end of Communism, their struggle might have seemed hopeless and pathetic. Although they did not state it explicitly, it is clear that they distinguished themselves from the common people, who submitted more willingly to Communism, and sacrificed less in resisting it.

Havel and Michnik expressed deep disillusion with the unfolding of the events after the fall of Communism. They regretted that the many sacrifices they had to make personally, suffering harassment from Communist authorities and deep solitude, only amounted in the end to a new society where getting rich seemed to have become the new ideal. "We changed the human rights charter into a credit card," wrote Michnik.[8]

Both he and Havel expressed in very negative words their point of view on present times: "uncanny," "dishonest," They perceived a free-for-all, egoistic way of life. Michnik compared their era with another period where money and indifference for the public good seemed to rule: Restoration France, as it was described by Stendhal.[9]

Havel and Michnik feared that the resurgence of Russian imperialism, combined with the people's cynicism and apathy, might lead them once more to yield to the tyranny of a strong man.

Yet when asked what alternative they would have imagined, both Havel and Michnik recognized that their primary goal was to put an end to the Communist regime imposed by Soviet forces. A common Enemy was the unifying factor. The restoration of private property and private initiative was a logical part of their project.

The end of a common threat is enough to produce sweeping changes in the way the people who faced it perceive each other and are perceived by others.

In 2010, a copper mine collapsed in Copiapó, Chile. Thirty-three miners managed to survive underground without any contact with the surface for seventeen days. They remained half a mile underground for sixty-nine days before excavators reached them. Their rescue was made a national priority by Sebastián Piñera, the Chilean President. The event was mediatized worldwide.

The audience sympathized with their plight. The Chilean President as well as some of the miners were later invited to give speeches in many countries. All were offered money from private donators on top of pensions. Some were given homes. Others were offered new jobs.

One could have expected the miraculously rescued miners to live happy lives ever after, and to stay on friendly terms for the rest of their days, but it turned out this is not how they managed. Some of them acknowledged they envied other survivors who made more money out of their sudden celebrity. Some declared they felt they had been taken advantage of.

Egoistic motives and focus on material success became dominant in the narratives of their lives after the rescue.[10]

The rise of bipolarization favors a sense of competition to enlist ordinary people. It favors a desire to produce and redistribute more than the other side. Equalitarianism rises, and so do production and redistribution. Bipolarization, equalitarianism, production and redistribution all change together. Their variations are synchronized. And so, when bipolarization declines again, so do equalitarianism, and the will to produce and redistribute more.

18. Producing and Distributing to Overcome

Bipolarization, production and redistribution rise and decline together.

This could be observed, for example, in the United States during the twentieth century.

The variations of international bipolarization that affected the United States during the period are reflected by federal military spending as a percentage of the gross domestic product (GDP), from 1910 to 2007 (*Figure 16*).[1] Variations in production are indicated by changes in real GDP.[2] Variations in the redistribution of wealth are illustrated by the share of total income, including capital gains, going to the 90 percent least wealthy Americans.[3]

The underlying trends in variations are visualized more easily in five-year mean military spending as a percentage of GDP compared to the 1910–2002 average; five-year mean change in GDP relative to the 1930–2010 average; and five-year mean change in income share going to the 90 percent least wealthy Americans.

The same long-term trends appear regarding all three indicators. They reveal three different periods, with similar long-term variations in military spending, production and redistribution: the first from c. 1919 to c. 1930, the second from c. 1930 to c. 1944, the third from c. 1945 to c. 2005.

First, from c. 1919 to c. 1930, international conflicts declined, as did production and redistribution. Between 1914 and 1918, during the major international conflict later known as World War I, the United States had joined Great Britain, France and their allies to defeat Germany and its allies. After the war, as external threats were felt to be extremely low, the US adopted a policy of isolation. Military spending decreased relative to the GDP until c. 1930. The end of that first phase is marked by a considerable contraction of the GDP, while income distribution became much more unequal.

During a second period, from c. 1930 to c. 1945, international bipolarization, production and redistribution all rose sharply. Hostile regimes like the Soviet Union, Germany and Japan embarked on an expansionist and aggressive foreign policy. Their neighbors in Europe and Asia were increasingly unable to contain them. The isolationist policy of the US became less and less credible. The nation found itself at war at the end of 1941. As a result, military spending doubled from 1928 to 1938 and multiplied by more than thirty between 1938 and 1944.

Production followed a similar upward trend over the period. While the real US GDP had contracted on average annually by -7.4 percent between 1930 and 1933, it rose by 6.9 percent on average from 1934 to 1938 and by 12.8 percent on average from 1939 to 1944. Likewise, while income distribution had become more unequal before 1930, it stabilized between c. 1930 and c. 1940. Between c. 1940 and c. 1944 it became dramatically more equal. The share of income going to the 90 percent least wealthy Americans rose from 55 percent to 67 percent.

During a third period, from c. 1945 to c. 2005, the long-term trend reverted. International bipolarization slowly declined and so did economic growth and wealth equality.

During the first decades that followed World War II, external threats seemed to remain exceptionally high. The US definitely renounced their isolationist stance and led a permanent international alliance. They mobilized to resist the conquest of the world by the communist bloc. Military spending remained far above pre-WWII levels. The Cold War between the US and its allies and the Soviet Union and its satellites knew intense but localized conflicts in Korea (c. 1950–1953) and in Vietnam (c. 1965–1973). Neat temporary increases in military spending correspond. After a short post-WWII depression, GDP growth became rapidly positive again while income distribution reached its 1945 level again in 1953. Real GDP and income equality rose with both the Korean War and the Vietnam War.

However, in the longer term, international bipolarization was slowly declining, as reflected by the long-term constant decline in US military spending. It went from an average 10.3 percent of GDP in the 1950s to an average 3.9 percent in the 1990s. Likewise, real GDP growth was on average 3.3 percent from 1946–1979 and only 2.7 percent from 1980–2010. Income distribution remained fairly constant until 1980. From that year onwards, it rapidly became more concentrated.

This reflected the long end of the Cold War. Although various dates between 1985 and 1991 are recorded as the official end of the Cold War, the data analyzed here accredits the possibility that in the US, the idea underlying the Cold War – that Moscow's hand was behind all revolutions and conflicts, expanding a communist bloc – weakened much earlier. It must have declined in the early 1970s, when rival communist states – China and the USSR – seemed posed to confront each other, and was certainly dead after the 1979 Islamic Revolution in Iran, which challenged both the USSR and the USA.

All three periods: the 1920s, 1930-1945 and 1945-2005 illustrate a correlation between changes in international bipolarization, in production and in income distribution.

Similar trends can be observed over the same periods in other countries whose populations were mobilized by the same international bipolarization. Similar cyclical trends have also been observed in these countries over the previous centuries.

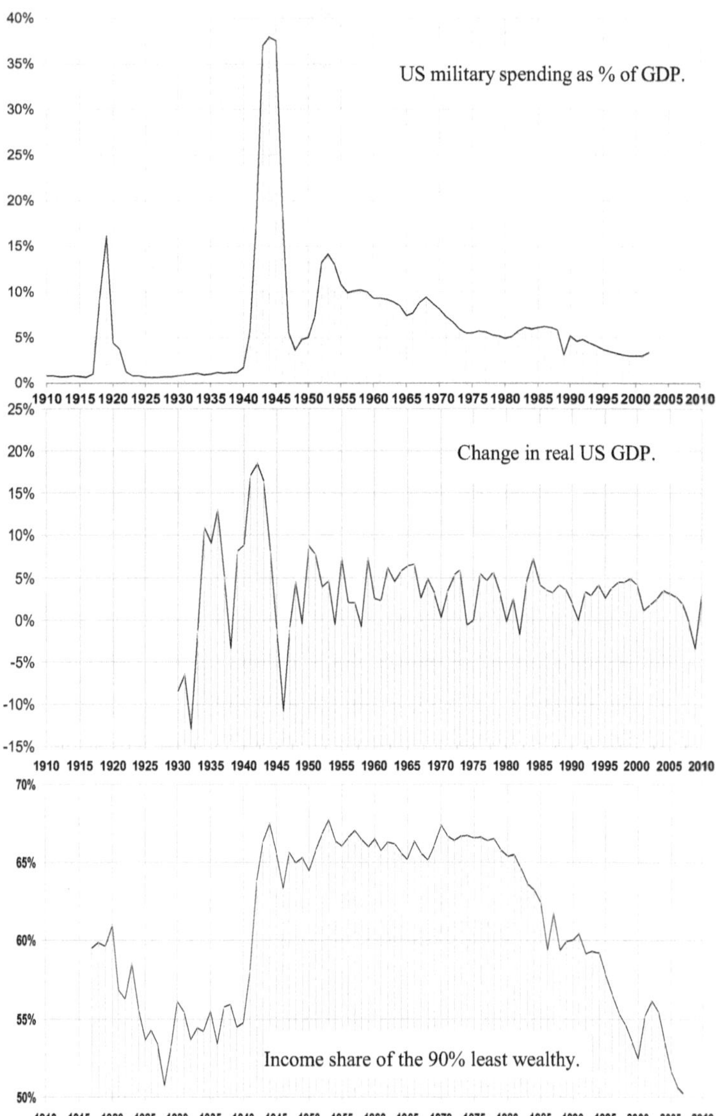
40%
35%
30%
25%
20%
15%
10%
5%
0%
US military spending as % of GDP.
1910 1915 1920 1925 1930 1935 1940 1945 1950 1955 1960 1965 1970 1975 1980 1985 1990 1995 2000 2005 2010
25%
20%
15%
10%
5%
0%
-5%
-10%
-15%
Change in real US GDP.
1910 1915 1920 1925 1930 1935 1940 1945 1950 1955 1960 1965 1970 1975 1980 1985 1990 1995 2000 2005 2010
70%
65%
60%
55%
50%
Income share of the 90% least wealthy.
1910 1915 1920 1925 1930 1935 1940 1945 1950 1955 1960 1965 1970 1975 1980 1985 1990 1995 2000 2005 2010

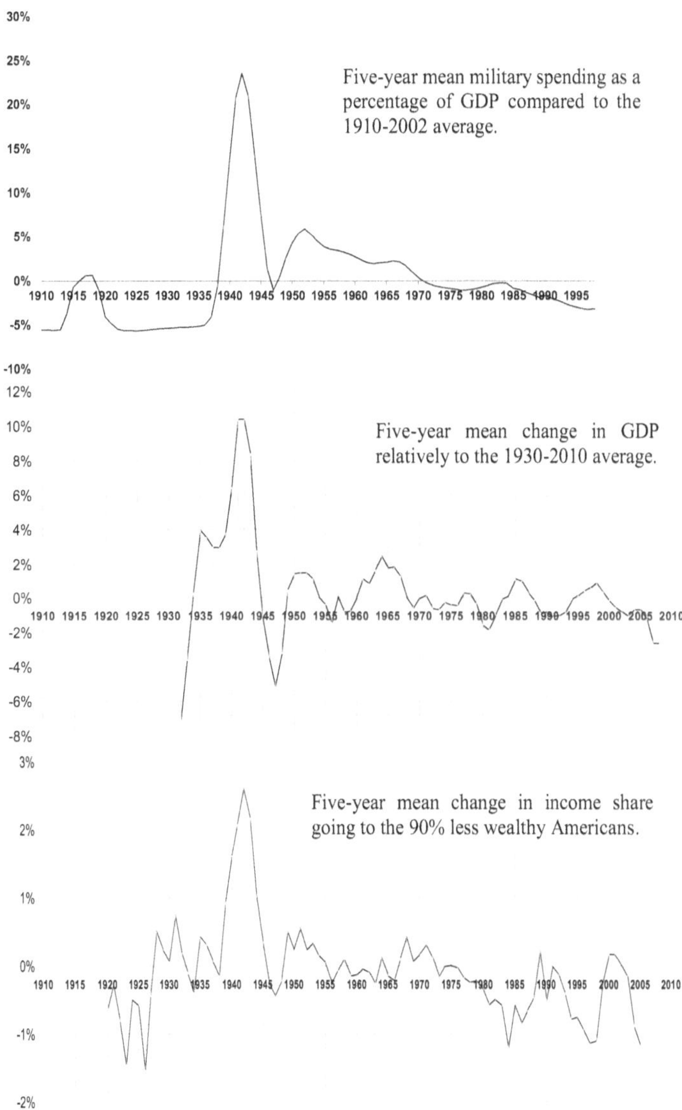

Figure 16. Economic Trends in 20th c. USA.

*

In the early 1920s Nikolai Kondratiev claimed he had found evidence that a law ruled all human activities. He had indeed observed long-term international correlations between upswings and downturns in a wide range of data. These observations concerned agricultural and industrial prices and volumes, wages, international trade, innovations, conflicts and even the rhythm of expansion of the international society concerned by these correlated movements.[4]

Kondratiev found these results by analyzing variations in the prices and volumes produced and traded for commodities such as coal, pig iron or cotton. He also analyzed variations in labor wages, interest rates or the prices of securities. He was able to draw on statistical publications from France, Britain and the United States starting in the late eighteenth century. From the 1870s onwards the series analyzed also covered most countries of Western Europe.

Kondratiev observed that the upswings and downturns corresponded to long cycles. According to his observations, a first long-term cycle started in Western Europe and in the US in the late 1780s. It peaked around 1815 and ended in the late 1840s. A second started at that point, peaked in the early 1870s and declined until the 1890s. A third cycle peaked in the late 1910s.

The three peaks observed by Kondratiev thus coincided with major international conflicts. The years 1810–1815 marked the heights of the Napoleonic Wars all over Europe. The period 1870–1875 immediately followed the Prussian victories over Austria and France, the final stages of Italian unification and the aftermath of the American Civil War. The years 1914–1920 are those of World War I and of those following civil wars in Central and Eastern Europe (Figure 17).

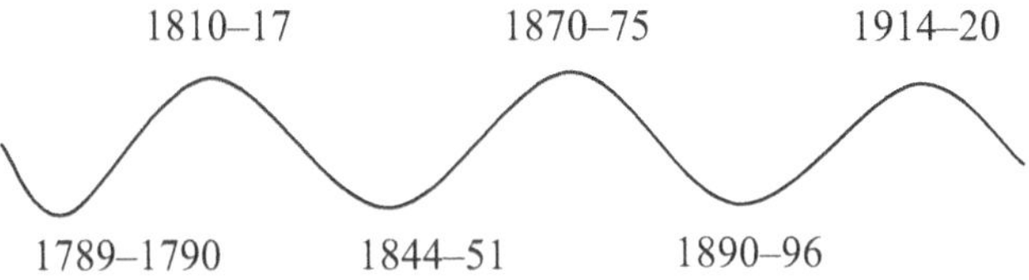

Figure 17. "Long-wave" peaks and troughs (Kondratiev).

Joshua Goldstein observed correlations similar to the ones detected by Kondratiev, but on a considerably longer time span: 1495–1980.[5] He indicated the following cycles for prices in Western Europe prior to the period covered by Kondratiev:

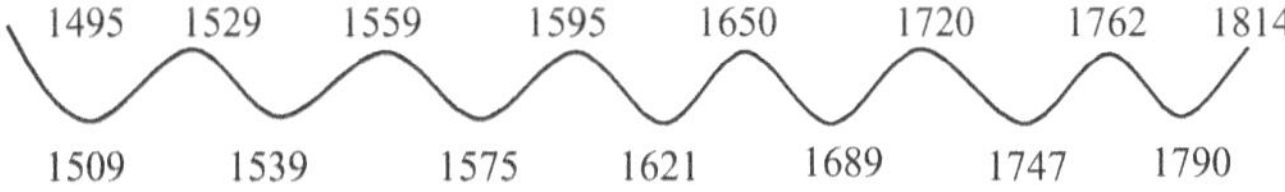

Figure 18. "Long-wave" peaks and troughs (Goldstein).

Kondratiev supposed that the correlations he observed were too regular and all-encompassing to be ascribed to independent, unconnected circumstances. "We have really to deal with a law governing the events."[6] This was a fundamental scientific problem. There was no explanation or "theory"[7] to account for it. Not long after the publication of his works, Kondratiev was deported and executed by the Stalinist regime. The problem remained unsolved until now.

V

The Competition for Distinction

Companions recognize each other. They know each one of them is more than an ordinary person. Each one finds in their companions reassurance, a confirmation about intimate intuitions, a promise of a superior destiny.

But the more people spend time with companions, the more they also encounter opportunities to doubt them; over time companions seem less aware of the Enemy's presence than the one is. Each one desires not to be confined to an exclusive relation. They want to find more companions.

Each one is thus aware that companions may be doubtful too. One demands the presence and attention of dedicated companions, and the least movement in another direction, the least look, the least word can be feared, noticed and resented. Any contact, any exchange, however banal or short-lived, can imply a preference for someone over someone else.

Any time spent with each other is therefore an exchange of favors. Companions distinguish each other. By turning towards someone else, they downgrade their companions who are bound to react with hostility. Being so marginalized is felt to be an impediment in the struggle against the Enemy and is interpreted as his design. By getting closer to someone else each one implicitly accepts an alliance with that person against a former companion. Alliances are inherently unstable.

Each one is aware of the general competition for distinction. People seek to outcompete each other. Companions are allies but also rivals. No relation is devoid of ambiguity. The desire to be distinguished is only matched by the fear of being downgraded *(19 – Allies and* Rivals*)*.

Anyone desires to be considered at least as much as anyone else among their peers. But, except in day-dreaming, no one can ask for more, for no one else would consent to it. Alliances are based on reciprocal favors, and, when many people are involved, on equality and rules applying to all alike *(20 – Reciprocal Favors)*.

Companions are the only source of truth and the only source of people's worth, in every sense of the word. Each one is only worth what companions think and say. An asset is only as valuable as companions desire it to be. Trade and investments must follow alliances *(21 – To Prove One's Worth)*.

An exchange may well trigger hostility from someone who is not privy to it. Accepting an exchange is taking a risk, but not accepting it is taking the opposed risk. The person that is refused an exchange may also react with hostility.

Companions who succeed better than others arouse envy. Less favored people want to fight back and destroy their wealth and power. The desire to be distinguished inevitably generates shifting bipolar alliances. As a result, prices and volumes traded are cyclical, they must follow shifts in alliances *(22 – In Business like in* Warfare*)*.

In fact, all conflicts stem from rivalries among companions. People do not pick up adversaries among people they do not know. They may plunder, enslave and kill foreigners on occasion. But they engage in lasting alliances and conflicts with companions only.

Allies are driven to turn against each other, especially after a general victory or defeat, despite their desire to the contrary. Eventually, the desire to be distinguished must trigger another general bipolarization.

19. Allies and Rivals

When they find companions who support their ideas, each one is tempted to believe they are meant to play a decisive role. Companions never seem to be plainly aware of the threats that loom and of the urgency to act. Deep inside, each one desires to be chosen as the leader.

But no companion would ever consent to that promotion. They reserve it for themselves. They are allies and rivals at the same time.

Each one dreams of convincing companions by performing bold, exceptional deeds. One also imagines that rivals would discredit themselves and reveal themselves motivated by ordinary, narrow, egoistic interests. Each one thus knows that one's ambitions could be presented as selfish and insists on the contrary, on sacrifices made for the common cause.

In 1998 I interviewed four people, four friends, about an event that had taken place eight years earlier, the opening of the first school in Alsace teaching as much in German than in French. I interviewed them separately and all of them gave me strikingly converging versions of what had happened. All four spontaneously mentioned the other three. They presented them as companions, fellow activists promoting the teaching of German in Alsace. Each one recognized that the other three had been personally involved and had played an important role.

Their account differed only in one respect: each one claimed the decisive role, in substance saying that without their own individual initiatives the school would not have opened. They had shown the way to the other three.

Each one desires to be distinguished, recognized by their companions as a superior being, and destined to be the sole hero. And so no one would consent to elevate a companion above themselves. People can only day-dream that some special circumstance will indisputably distinguish them and reveal they play a unique role. This influences fiction.

The action in the movie *Master and Commander* takes place in 1805: "Napoleon is Master of Europe… only the British fleet stands before him." Capitan Aubrey's frigate, the *Surprise*, has been dispatched by the British Admiralty to "capture, burn or destroy" the *Acheron*, a French privateer en route to the Pacific. The mission seems at first of secondary importance but the *Acheron* reveals itself to be a large, well-manned ship. Lieutenant Thomas Pullings concludes: "such a heavy frigate in the Pacific… could tip the balance of war in Napoleon's favor." The *Surprise*, alone and facing a much heavier ship, will have to save the world from tyranny.[1]

In fiction, a particularly distinguishing circumstance is to be a last action hero, the one who arrives on the field of battle when the Enemy is about to win, when all companions have given up, when "there is no more hope," to quote from the trailer of the *Captain Future* TV anime movie.

At the end of *The Secret of the Swordfish,* Blake and Mortimer distinguish themselves in such circumstances and save the world.[2] The Yellow Empire has conquered the planet; only the last base in the "free world" still resists. At the very last moment, when the Enemy has discovered and penetrated the secret base itself, Blake and Mortimer successfully assemble and fly the *Swordfish*, a revolutionary airplane. Their new weapon completely reverses the situation. The base is saved and the world is rapidly liberated.

As in the *Secret of the Swordfish*, being a last-action hero often implies possession of a special object. One famous example of this specific distinguishing circumstance is found in the many variants of the legend of King Arthur, when he is recognized by all Britons as their king because alone he can detach the Sword in the Stone from the rock.

Each one desires to be distinguished by their companions. Each one may imagine similar desires in companions and a fear to be downgraded for being selfish.

The desire to be distinguished and the fear of being downgraded can also be observed when companions reward high deeds. The laureates are always reluctant to accept them. They insist on the sacrifices they made for the common cause. This tendency has no other source than the fear of being downgraded, of appearing like a materialistic, ordinary person rather than being safely identified as one of the selfless warriors.

Laureates fear that the "distinctions" they receive may be interpreted as compensations, so that far from being distinguished, the laureate is in fact downgraded, presented as an ordinary, egoistic and materialistic person that acted with a view to obtaining something in exchange for their actions. By associating oneself with companions and denying compensation, laureates seek to prevent their downgrading.

For example, one laureate of the René Schickele Prize, awarded by defenders of the German language in Alsace, complained upon receiving the prize that her dedication to the cause has lost her many friends. She emphasized her sacrifices.

The characteristic reluctance to be rewarded for high deeds can also be illustrated by the comments made in September 2011 when President Obama awarded the Medal of Honor, the nation's highest award for valor, to a former Marine "who ignored orders to stay put and fought his way five times into an ambush in an Afghan ravine." The Marine helped save several comrades and also recovered bodies. The President took care to present the laureate as "a selfless example of a citizen at his best…" He quoted Dakota confessing, "'I didn't think I was going to die. I knew I was.'" The President also described a man who was reluctant to accept the Medal. The laureate himself downplayed the importance of the distinction and of the high deeds, and underlined that many others may be equally meriting. "It may be a platform for representation of the guys who are out there fighting every day," he said in a telephone interview before the award ceremony. "My story is one of millions, and the others aren't often told."[3]

The risk of one's distinctions being turned into compensation brings about the desire of an "ultimate sacrifice," one that, it is imagined, could not be contested because there would be no possible compensation, like giving one's life in combat. It appears as the most straightforward way to be distinguished and, indeed, many such ends have been praised.

For instance, in Shakespeare's play, King Henry V considers it an honorable alternative to victory. Another example is Benjamin West's painting of British General James Wolfe's death in 1759 during the decisive and victorious Battle of Québec against the French. West represented Wolfe at the foot of the British flag in a position similar to that of the Christ deposed from the cross, evoking to a Christian public Wolfe's elevation by his sacrifice. The scene seemed to have moved deeply Admiral Horatio Nelson who wished for himself a comparable end. His will was later executed and he was also painted by West, lying down, mortally wounded on the bridge of the flagship Victory on October 21, 1805, off Cape Trafalgar, in the decisive battle against the French and Spanish fleets (*Figure 19*).

The same ideal could of course be observed on the side of the adversaries, the French. They had made their national anthem the *War Song for the Army of the Rhine* by Rouget de Lisle, better known as *La Marseillaise*. The song contains significant lines:

> We are much less jealous of surviving [our elders]
> Than of sharing their coffins
> We shall have the sublime pride
> Of avenging or joining them.[4]

But even the ultimate sacrifice can be downgraded, reduced to a self-interested move. Many have imagined that companions fallen in the line of duty would find retribution for their high deeds in the afterlife, for instance in the arms of beautiful she-angels, as in the Germanic Valhalla, or in Anne-Louis Girodet-Trioson's painting Ossian Receiving the Ghosts of the French Heroes (*Figure 20*).

No high deed, however extreme, can be a guarantee that companions will distinguish one of them above the others. They can never do so of course for each one supremely desires such an elevation for themselves.

Figure 19. The Death of Nelson *by Benjamin West (detail, 1806).*[5]

Figure 20. Ossian Receiving the Ghosts of the French Heroes *by Anne-Louis Girodet-Trioson (detail, 1801).*[6]

20. Reciprocal Favors

The desire to be distinguished makes each one aware that their peers want the same. One fears that companions may accept new alliances that would distinguish them alone. The fear of being left behind is as strong as the desire to be distinguished.

The inherent instability of relationships is a cause of anxiety that inspires in reaction an ideal of exclusive alliances, everlasting love and faithfulness to promises, not only in day-dreaming, or in romantic literature, but also in actual relations.

This means that actual alliances demand reciprocity, equality and rules.

Fellowship is based on the ideal of reciprocity. Any favor demands a favor in return. "There is no free gift,"[1] whether it is a good or a service or a position. Gifts and favors create obligations. They must be exchanged.

A particularly spectacular type of exchange was reported by Marcel Mauss. It took place sometime in the nineteenth century in the Melanesian Islands. Its goal was to establish an international alliance. It implied complex exchanges such as the ones which could be observed between families when they celebrated weddings, but on a much grander scale.

On this occasion a whole people collaborated in producing and accumulating distinctive goods designed to be distributed to allies during an overseas expedition. The gifts received in exchange were brought back and redistributed by the lords to the dependents and allies who had provided the goods.

During the festivities marking the arrival of the new allies on the island, mock attacks were organized to signify the absence of hostility and the search for friendship and alliance.[2] But they were also a reminder of the possible consequences should the gifts offered not be properly reciprocated.[3]

To return gifts was considered a duty, the breach of which was imagined to have terrible consequences, possibly death itself. It is easy to understand why. People whose gifts were not reciprocated were deemed to be misallied. They were downgraded because they had accepted to be regarded as equals with people who were not worthy of them. The only way to avoid being in turn downgraded by their other allies was to persuade them to make war on the culprit and his family or nation and punish them.

The same dynamics of exchanges, alliances and conflicts can be observed during potlatches. A potlatch is an annual gathering and religious festival that took place – and still takes place – among many people of North America and Siberia: the Kwakiutl and Tsimshian in British Columbia, the Haida and Tlingit in Alaska, and the Koryak and Chukchi in Siberia.

A potlatch may last all winter. The groups gathered compete to offer the most magnificent feasts and to make the most valuable gifts and sacrifices. The generosity that the groups display determines who can marry who, who can be allied with whom. A person or a tribe that cannot offer in return more than they received must accept subordination. In the most extreme cases, people can even be reduced into slavery.[4] Thus there is a reckless competition to make the most costly gifts to the living and to the gods. It generates large coalitions that produce the greatest possible accumulation of goods. No one dares to refuse a gift. It could have the most extreme consequence. It would only be interpreted as a way to deny the giver any distinction, and it would be a possible cause of war.[5]

A favor that is not returned properly is a humiliation, a downgrading. Between companions, any favor asks for a favor in return.

When the exchanges take place between more than two companions, simple reciprocity does not suffice. Favors exchanged between companions imply objects and positions that symbolize equality among all of them. The services granted, the objects given and the distinctions awarded must be all the same. At the same time they must also be special, different from those produced for ordinary people. They must be exclusive to companions.

The famous Round Table is such an object, a symbol of exclusivity, reciprocity and equality among companions. The legendary King Arthur would have gathered the most famous and courageous knights to defend his realm. All would have been seated at the Round Table which would have had that shape precisely so that no one would have occupied a better or a lesser place, each one being exactly at the same distance from the others. By contrast, oblong tables allow the placing of the most distinguished guests at the end or in the middle. At a round table, no such distinction is possible. All are seated equally. Many knights' orders used round tables fashioned after the legendary one.[6]

For the same reason, many orders of chivalry gave exactly similar medals and symbols to their members, either the most famous Order of the Golden Fleece or the Order of la Jarretière or the Order of the Bath. Equality applied to the ceremonies as well as to the goods. The initiation into the order, for instance, must be as similar as possible for all applicants.

Companions often enjoy similar positions. They would for example be represented in a hall of fame, a room or building established especially to honor individuals distinguished for a superior contribution to the common cause. Halls of fame appear in quite various settings. The Office of the Gaelic Language in Dublin possessed such a room: former chairpeople's portraits hang on the walls, not unlike former headmasters in the Headmaster's Office in Hogwarts. Likewise, the headquarters of the Paris Chamber of Commerce contains a room where the walls are covered with portraits of the former Chairmen. There is even a highly select Society of the former Chairmen of the Chamber.

A more grandiose example of a hall of fame is the Walhalla, the building erected near Regensburg in the 1830s in the classic form of a sacred temple by King Ludwig I of Bavaria to gather the busts of all the great ancestors of the German nation. King Ludwig's own bust eventually found its way to the Walhalla, of course. In the emulation between European national movements in the nineteenth century, the Walhalla became a German national symbol like the French and Italian Pantheons, and Westminster Abbey in Britain, all of which were dedicated to the great ancestors of their respective nations. In such a hall of fame, all companions finally share a common position.

When more than two people are involved, reciprocity and equality imply common rules. Like the exchange of objects and positions, the ediction and enforcement of common rules is made to reinforce the suggestion that the people to which the rules apply are a distinguished group of peers and allies rather than competitors and rivals.

A rule is indeed enounced with the expectation that all people will follow it, and act accordingly, in the same way, equally. Furthermore, rules tend to forbid actions and gestures that suggest that someone takes unfair advantage from a situation. Finally, compliance with rules is extolled and valorized as part of a common heritage. Those who follow the rules are presented as distinguished people.

Rules are different from habits, even if both suggest regularity. Habits are personal and, in the absence of rules touching the actions, nothing should prevent someone from altering their ways. Rules, by contrast, are collective. People have no choice; if they do not comply, they signal themselves for exclusion from the group.

Table manners developed in Western Europe since the Middle-Ages are an excellent example of rules. There are apparently so many of them yet they actually all have the same logic. They are designed to produce a sense of a high degree of coordination and thereby a sense of equality at table, a sense that guests do not distinguish themselves from each other, but only from those who are not at the table.

The rules indeed possess a specific, stereotyped form: "it is polite to do so" or "it is rude to act in such way." They are impersonal and general. They apply to all indifferently. Their form suggests that no one can change them or decide not to follow them.

They are also expressed as binary propositions. Guests who behave properly are implicitly recognized as belonging to the "good society." a superior type of people. Those who do not comply are excluded from that category.[7]

They aim to suggest that all people at the table are peers. They tend to prohibit any action that may distinguish one of the guests from the others. They prohibit attracting too much attention to oneself, or not paying attention to the others, or eating a disproportionate share of the food, or not eating one's proper share, or even suggesting that one might desire to engage in any of these reproved actions.[8]

It is thus prohibited and seen as impolite to reach over someone to pick up food. Items must be asked for or, even better, proposed to the other guests without them asking. Plates received must be passed on. It is prohibited to pour only one's own drink. It is also prohibited to talk with food in one's mouth. All these rules converge in ensuring that people all eat converging amounts, at a similar rhythm. Eating too slowly or too rapidly or serving divergent amounts to the various guests without seeking proper permission to do so is therefore also considered quite impolite.

Table manners also prohibit some guests suggesting that they may enjoy the meal and benefit from it more than others. They prohibit eating noisily or eating without closing one's mouth or licking one's fingers. They prohibit things such as making too much noise or speaking out of turn.

Table manners finally aim to repress any gesture that might induce anger and aggression in guests. Therefore, they also repress gestures that may directly suggest aggressiveness, like the excessive use of knifes[9]. "Host" and "guest" originally both had a much more evident ambivalence, meaning both could be a potential ally and a potential foe. The rise of rules like table manners, designed to suppress social tensions and facilitate alliances, paradoxically erased the original ambivalence of the words which justified them. What remains is a sense that table manners distinguish the "good society."

People that uphold rules distinguish each other. They are therefore constantly monitoring for trespassers and recognize each other as having the right to judge others. Rules can be enforced by groups even in the absence of formal tribunals and sanctions. Gossip and the threat of exclusion are the most common form of enforcement.

Gossip, for example, plays a central role in *Stromboli*, a film by Roberto Rossellini[10] where Ingrid Bergman plays a newlywed. The couple settles on the Island of Stromboli, where the husband was born. She is rapidly marginalized and subjected to gossip because she is too beautiful and adopts a way of life different from the rest of the village: she paints her home in bright colors rather than in black and white, wears a nice dress, etc. Villagers try to persuade her husband that she is a lusty, unfaithful wife. They resent that she seeks to distinguish herself and has no respect for local traditions. They feel despised by her when they had admitted her in their midst. She eventually tries to escape and kills herself.

Bergman too was the subject of malevolent gossip when *Stromboli* was released in the US. She had started a scandalous extramarital affair with Rossellini. Furthermore, Bergman was a recent Swedish immigrant in the US, and Rossellini was thought to be a communist. It was 1950, at the apex of the Cold War. Innuendo had it that Bergman was a traitor not only to Hollywood and to morality, but also to the Free World. She had crossed too many lines. There were rules, even for a star.

Rules like table manners apply in the context of small groups which essentially regulate themselves. Their underlying goal, promoting equality and reciprocity among people, can be found in all rules, even the most formal that apply to the signature and sanction of contracts or of international treaties.

One learns it is necessary in many cases to follow the rules in order to please companions, but the temptation is always there to disobey. No one wants to be "rational" like ordinary people are imagined to be, and indefinitely submit to an order. The desire to be distinguished generates as much the desire to be above the law, the pleasure to break the rules, the attraction of mischief as does the desire to be with companions. And the experience of instability in companionship elicits as much an ideal of eternal friendship and love, as cynicism, whereby all relations are imagined as mere calculations, and the whole life a self-interested theater of pretenses. No relation can stay infinitely unthreatened and no rule can stay forever unchallenged.

21. To Prove One's Worth

Companions distinguish each other. They recognize each other as companions, as distinguished people and elevate each other above the common lot. Anyone's worth depends on companions.

Companions are the source of all truths. They distinguish each other. They make and unmake someone's "reputation," which in different contexts can be named "credit," "fame," "valor" or "honor." This principle is for example illustrated by the different meanings of the word "credit": credit is fundamentally the "influence or power derived from enjoying the confidence of another or others." From this derives the "good name, esteem, financial or commercial trustworthiness," and therefore "an amount or sum placed at a person's disposal" or "the balance in a person's favor in an account."[1]

Companions are the only source of people's worth, in every sense of the word. They are the only source of truth; each one is only worth what companions think and say. Likewise, an asset is only as valuable as companions desire it to be.

The same beliefs, and, in consequence, the same dynamics of association and conflicts can be observed regardless of the number of people involved, the complexity of the exchange networks, the exchangeability or "liquidity" of the assets traded, the modalities of the exchange and retribution.

Trade and investments must follow alliances.

Any exchange, any purchase, any investment is always made with a view to obtain a better return than most competitors. Exchanging and investing proceed of the same logic, and pursue the same goal. When someone accepts to exchange with someone else, both persons invest in that relationship. Exchanges create bonds. The people who are part of the exchange become companions.

The verb to "invest" has retained much of its original meaning, which was closely associated with mutual distinction. It literally meant to put someone in a "vest," that is to give them a new and specific role, to elevate them to a new status, a new position. These different meanings are nowadays retained by the verb "to invest." Someone may be invested "into" an order of companions, "as a member" of that order, or may be invested "with" powers, or simply "invested" when chosen to occupy a given office or function...

Any investment is first and foremost an investment in a relationship. It is primarily based on trust. Fellowship is the primary asset, the one from which all other derive.

Each one is aware of this. Exchanging with companions distinguishes one from ordinary people. By extension, distinguished people are always credited with being well introduced in select circles. Being distinguished, being well connected, being influential and being powerful are therefore spontaneously associated; their equivalence is undisputed.

Each one is much aware of the general competition for distinction. Any gift is an investment in a relationship. But no one could openly present their companions and friends as mere assets. There is a universal desire to distinguish true friendship and elevated, disinterested types of exchanges between worthy, noble persons – from calculations and base trading between ordinary, interested people.

Let me cite an illustration regarding this notion. An episode took place sometime in the nineteenth century in the Trobriand Islands, during a ceremony designed to mark the conclusion of an international alliance. Gifts were brought by the visiting head of state to his counterpart. The main gift, which was particularly precious and offered in the most solemn manner, had nonetheless to be presented as of no consequence, with much protestations of regrets and a profusion of excuses. This attitude was a particularly marked way to pretend that no gift or favor was expected in return, when in fact, this was obviously the case. But to have pretended otherwise would have made the visitor a mere merchant who sought an exchange and a benefit. Likewise it would have downgraded the host who took part in the exchange. It would have been "gimwali," "ordinary" trade, not "kula," "aristocratic" exchanges.[2] All participants to the ceremony were well aware of it. So the act was far from lacking basis and significance. Even if it might, at first glance, have seemed a little paradoxical and perhaps slightly hypocritical, it was the sincere desire to achieve the alliance that had dictated it. And as such, it was well received by the host. It was, in the words of Western diplomacy, a necessary protestation of good faith.

Discussing the value of the goods exchanged would be regarded as utterly lacking in nobility and degrading in any society. It was of course completely impossible during the potlatch[3] as it would be in other high-level exchanges. Calculations about wealth are always considered to be proper to lower people. The credit of honorable people should not depend on the way they accumulate wealth.

Likewise, in the early twenty-first century, powerful business people distinguish themselves notably by claiming that they "give back to the community." This type of actions is, implicitly, accessible only to very wealthy and successful

236

people who recognize each other as superior capital, socially and financially. "Giving back to the community" may well be regarded as a way to "show off" and, in many ways, it is just that. However, it implies a strict code of honor.

Those who do not accept "giving back" or, at least, those who do not give enough back, are excluded. I was once privy to such a corridor conservation. The chairman of a non-profit organization explained to his visitor that a celebrity they both hobnobbed with would henceforth not be accepted in their club because that person had made it a habit of billing his services to the non-profit organization as would have been normal had it been a for-profit corporation. This selfish and greedy behavior, both agreed, could be tolerated no further. And the banishment was indeed carried out. Both men were ruthless businesspeople. "Giving back to the community" was just another way to distinguish themselves. But this did not mean they would just accept any behavior.

In fact, there is no difference between ordinary trade and aristocratic trade. The difference is only an illusion. Can any trader nakedly pretend they are not particularly honored to do business with their client? Certainly not. Offering a drink to the client, proposing an extra service for free, taking time to discuss community affairs on the marketplace with local clients, or simply offering a smile when the simplicity of the exchange does not allow more – it is all plainly part of the art of the deal. It is wholly part of the honor of tradespeople to act pleasantly and to make believe their clients are special guests. Only a very disgruntled merchant would not attempt to do so. And they would probably not remain active for very long, for who would recommend such a shop?

A senior manager in the financial industry summarized his trade in these words:

You have to pretend you offer something very special, that the others do not. You cannot just pretend you offer the same thing as everyone else, only just a little better. That will not do. If you do not pretend your products are exceptional, they will seem to be less interesting than the products of your competitors.

Companions are the source of all distinction, of all worth. They are the judges, and they are also the competitors. They are the ones that must be impressed, and one can only impress them with assets that they value too. People compete with the other people who can access the same types of goods and invest their wealth and credit in the same type of venture. Only these can be envisaged as potential allies. Only they are actual rivals.

No man tries to rival those who lived ten thousand years ago, or are about to be born, or are already dead; nor those who live near the Pillars of Hercules; nor those who, in his own opinion or in that of others, are either far inferior or superior to him... We envy those whose possession of or success in a thing is a reproach to us: these are our neighbors and equals.

Hence, Aristotle observed, the well-known saying: "Potters envy potters." This is confirmed by an anecdote provided by a friend who remembered a conversation with a top manager:

I suddenly realized this guy was making more in a year than I would in my entire life. But I am not even jealous. He has problems with investments I know nothing about. He can buy things I have no idea about. He told me that Audis are worth nothing and I should buy a Mercedes. As if I could buy a Mercedes...

People desire what their companions could desire too. They envy only what they could exchange with them. Rivalries tend to oppose people of similar ranks and material conditions.

This logic of competition through an accumulation of similar goods is well illustrated by the portraits made by Titian. Tiziano Vecellio, alias Titian (c. 1490–1576), was a famous painter who made a reputation from portraying high-status people. He was especially praised for his ability to paint beautifully detailed artifacts that evoked wealth, glory, prestigious distinctions and revealed the high social status of their subjects: silks, jewelry, gilded armors, ribbons, medals, etc. Being portrayed by Titian in turn became another sign of high rank.

Yet, the painter produced one portrait that differed markedly from his others. The man does not look upwards and sideways, like in the other portraits. No, he is not avoiding the gaze of the public in a display of superiority. Instead, he looks directly at the viewer, his equal. He is soberly dressed, in black. Only a minor detail gives us a clue as to who he might be. He wears a tiny pendant on a very thin necklace that barely shows at the opening of the coat. The pendant is in the form of a golden lamb. Only the initiated person knows that this is the badge of the Order of the Golden Fleece, the most exclusive of orders, a symbol of very high status. Only someone well introduced may recognize the portrait of Charles V, the Holy Roman Emperor, the most powerful man in the world of Titian. It features none of the expected signs of imperial power: no scepter, no crown, no globe.

This portrait defies the rules that applied to all others in Titian's work. It is distinct and more important than all others. We may understand the implicit logic behind the choices made: only Charles V did not need to enter into a competition with the princes of his time. In fact, by choosing not to indulge in a bashful display of ceremonial ornaments and artifacts, he distinguished himself far more than he ever could have otherwise. The portrait of his son, King Philip, all gold and royal symbols, is proof enough. Charles V sets himself in a category wholly apart by stripping himself from the material artifacts that other portraits accumulate.

The intention of Titian cannot be mistaken. Only one other portrait makes use of a similar simplicity. Once again, a man dressed in black harbors no other artifact than a discreet pendant. At the bottom of the canvas one may recognize a brush, the tools of a painter. It is the self-portrait of Titian. The similarity in treatment of both subjects is not a coincidence. The artist did not choose to portray his relatives and his dear friend, Pietro Aretino, with the same simple attires. Titian did not see himself as another aristocrat whose distinction rested on the accumulation of rare artifacts, in spite of the wealth he made out of his portraits. Deep inside, Titian saw himself as distinct, and superior, thanks to his mere talent.

Titian's work seemed to promote the notion that ownership was the essence of distinction. Yet, Titian's intimate desire was to elevate himself above ordinary materialism. This he kept to himself though. Only the gathering of all his portraits, something that would have been impossible in his lifetime, gives access to the secret hierarchy he composed.

However, his secret desire is shared by anyone in the public. This was illustrated by an imaginary anecdote narrated by a guide when I visited the exhibition.

Figure 21. Portrait of Charles V, *by Titian (detail, 1548).*[4]

Figure 22. Portrait of Alfonso d'Avalos, *by Titian (detail, 1533)*[5]

According to the guide, Emperor Charles V visited Titian's workshop. The painter was concentrating so hard that he did not hear his visitor coming. He inadvertently dropped a brush. The Emperor handed it back. The painter recognized the sovereign and protested. But the Emperor explained it was a natural mark of respect towards the painter. After all, there are many Emperors but only one Titian. Variants of the same anecdote exist about other artists. They only translate how universal the desire for distinction is. But other people than Charles V and Titian did not have the option of setting themselves apart. In buying a portrait by Titian, they sought to acquire an artifact that would cast them as a member of a prestigious group, and in order to achieve that, they had to display symbols of their wealth and power.

The value of an asset depends on the value companions ascribe to it. The value of a service is tied to the person that provides it. By extension, the value of any asset or good depends on the quality of its previous owners, including its maker. It also depends on the future owners, if they can be determined.

The value of assets is derived from that of their makers and owners. The value of an asset, tangible or not, is entirely tied to the reputation of their makers and previous owners. Personal credit goes to the goods.

For instance, an investor investing in a stock lends it their credit. Conversely, no assets can in themselves entirely explain the credit of a person or of a company. As any financial analyst knows, the value of a company is reflected not only in the numbers on its balance sheet; it is also the result of the "goodwill" of investors.

The relation between the value of an object and the status of its owner is much simpler to imagine when the owner is a very distinguished person and the object, as a result, can be one that is difficult to exchange. The value of Charlemagne's sword, *Joyeuse,* cannot be compared to any similar artifact; in fact, it is unique and therefore, as such, priceless. Likewise, the stone that is inserted in the Throne of Great Britain during coronations, has a specific value, which very much depends on how much one treasures the British monarchy, not that type of stone. Should the British monarchy end, and all memories of it, the stone might be regarded again as a stone like any other. For the time being, it is impossible to exchange it against another stone.

By contrast, any buyer or seller will have much less influence on the price of an asset in a deep, liquid market. For example, the price of an apartment in a big city does not depends much

242

on the tastes of an individual seller or buyer. Even if the potential buyers like the apartment a lot, they will generally not accept to pay much more than what "the market" ascribes to it. They anticipate selling it again. The propensity of other sellers and buyers to think alike only encourages them to think in that direction. Maynard Keynes famously compared investing in such assets to betting on a beauty contest. The actual beauty of the competitors has little importance. The opinion of the other bettors is decisive.[6]

The value of items with prestigious owners is difficult to estimate while items that could be possessed by many people are easily priced. The link between owner and value is therefore difficult to imagine, but it is all-important nonetheless.

Here is another way to imagine the relation: makers are the first owners of items. The way they make them has an impact on the item's value. For instance, all things equal, more standardized goods have less value, as they evoke ordinary, comparable, replaceable items and makers. This is why, for example, the Saint-Louis crystal tableware factory reverted in the 1840s from mechanized molding to hand-cutting after it initially moved in the other direction in the 1820s. Hand-cutting was more expansive but the goal was to move from premium tableware to luxury tableware that would be sold to aristocratic and royal palaces, with a much bigger margin. Hand-cut glasses were in that respect a decisive argument in positioning the Saint-Louis brand as a luxury brand; each glass could indeed be considered unique and due to the irreplaceable skills of a craftsperson. The calculation proved correct and the Saint-Louis factory still operates nowadays in the luxury tableware market. The same logic explains that luxury items are rarely displayed in shops with their prices for everyone to see. This would suggest that anyone can buy them. It would make them less distinctive.

The relation between the good's value and its owner's or producer's credit is less intuitive when the good is more standardized. But even very standardized goods designed for mass consumption can appeal to the buyer's desire to acquire a premium item. Their differentiation can be based on branding, pricing or design. Even currencies, the most standard of goods, have distinct values which depend entirely on the authorities that issue them and on the confidence they consequently inspire in buyers.

*

The value of an asset depends on the opinion of companions.

As a result, the general rise in fellowship and alliances, and of bipolarization, and the general rise of trade should therefore go together. This is indeed what was observed by Kondratiev on an international scale over many decades.[7]

A related observation was made by Paul Krugman. He noticed that in the twentieth century the largest trading nations competed the most in producing and trading a similar range of goods. This struck him as the opposite of John Stuart Mill's famous prediction: that trading nations would gain in specializing in the production of different types of goods. But it is also in line with the principle that people invest in assets that their competitors desire, produce and exchange.[8]

Another consequence of the principle that the value of an asset depends on the opinion of companions is that even in "advanced" and "industrialized" economies, even in places where a considerable number of people and organizations produce and trade, particular individual relations still have a decisive influence on exchanges. The laws presiding over exchanges are fundamentally the same when a great number of people are involved, or when few are. In reality there cannot be a situation like the one usually associated with "perfect competition" where all investors, buyers and sellers, would have access to the same information, and where no investors would have a disproportionate, specific influence over exchanges and prices.[9]

Grossman and Stieglitz have explained why perfect competition is impossible. There is an incentive to buy or sell only where people believe they can make a better investment than others. "Whenever there are differences in beliefs that are not completely arbitraged, there is an incentive to create a market." Conversely, no one would invest or exchange in a market where prices would reflect an information that all could equally access.[10]

22. In Business like in Warfare

Companions who succeed better than others arouse envy. Less favored people want to fight back and destroy their wealth and power.

But the desire to be distinguished may also lead companions to destroy the wealth of their peers in order to prevent their elevation sometime in future.

Either way the competition for distinction inevitably generates shifting bipolar alliances. Prices and volumes traded follow the shifts in alliances. They must be cyclical.

People never accept to be downgraded. They would never accept their companions to be elevated when they are not themselves. They are bound to retaliate against any such move, and the way they do only depends on the means available to them.

To illustrate: monkeys were lined up and given a fistful of little white pebbles. Seated in front of each of them, a human traded a little piece of cucumber for a white pebble. All monkeys accepted the exchange. After a while, one of the monkeys received, instead of cucumber, a little piece of apple, a morsel of choice. Upon seeing this all the other monkeys ceased the exchange and started throwing their pebbles in anger at their human counterparts. The humans felt that the monkeys had reacted as humans would have.

Sarah Brosnan and Frans de Waal[1] deduced from the event that "equal pay" was the goal pursued by the monkeys. This was not a correct deduction. Indeed, the one monkey who could accept to gain more than the others *did* and, as far as we know, the other ones might have done the same. "Equal pay" was merely the condition for the exchange to continue.

Only one goal might have been pursued by all monkeys: distinction. As long as all monkeys received the same return, all may have hoped to be distinguished. As soon as one of them was distinguished, all others lost interest in trade, and were apparently overwhelmed by anger. The observers were right to think that the monkeys had reacted as humans would have. At least in some respect. It is hard to know how humans would fare were they chained and subjected to the same conditions. Perhaps the less favored ones would have tried to talk their counterparts out of trading apples with the other ones. Perhaps they would have stopped trading without throwing the pebbles. Or maybe the monkeys were not really overwhelmed by anger but felt they had to put on a decent show to make their point.

Less fortunate rivals cannot always interrupt an exchange. In that case, they must seek compensation by different means, like destroying the winners' asset or at least trying to reduce their advantage if they can.

An experiment was conducted by Andrew Oswald and Daniel Zizzo with volunteers recruited at the University of Warwick. Each volunteer was given a sum of money and asked to place bets through computers. Groups of four were set up. Each volunteer could follow the gains made by the three other participants. In each group, the first two participants in alphabetical order were given unexplained gifts on top of their gains.

During the second phase of the experiment, Oswald and Zizzo allowed the participants to pay with their gains in order to reduce the gains of other players. Victims were then informed and could retaliate. A total of 62.6 percent of the participants chose to destroy some of their own assets in order to reduce the assets of other participants, and 20.6 percent of all gains were destroyed. The participants who had made the biggest gains, through bets and gifts, were more attacked than the others.[2]

These results reflect the competition for distinction that takes place in any group of competitors, especially when they can compare their assets and achievements and have no other possibility to improve their position than to attack more successful competitors. It is likely that the amounts destroyed could have been higher. Indeed, the price paid to destroy the assets of competitors rose with the amount already destroyed but could not exceed a quarter of the amount destroyed. It is likely that the price paid could have risen until it was almost equivalent to the amount destroyed. It could not have exceeded the amount destroyed, because the participants could not have gained relatively from such a move. However, the objective of the test was simply to disprove the "maximization" of gains as supposed under the rational choice theory. The destruction of some assets was enough to disprove it. The researchers did not feel it necessary to evaluate the maximum amount that could be destroyed.

It is remarkable that participants compared themselves to other participants rather than to the experiment organizers from whom they could have extracted much more cash. However, the organizers had created a number of circumstances likely to foster competition among participants. First, the sums gained were nominally "doblons," a currency created for the purpose of the experiment, which encouraged participants to compare themselves only with other participants, even if their gains were eventually converted and paid in real money. Second, computers were displaying the gains of all three other participants simultaneously during the experiment, which reinforced a sense of competition among participants. Third, the organizers also encouraged comparisons during the interviews that immediately preceded the destructive stage and fostered retaliation by disclosing the authors of aggression.

These experiments in fact isolate and encourage specific dynamics that spontaneously appear in any business relation, whether they concern only two people or a very large number of traders, as in financial and commodities markets.

Sooner or later some traders must decide to dissociate themselves from their associates in order to make certain that they gain more than most out of the bargain. Less fortunate traders cannot always retaliate.

Exchanges are inevitable. People must enter the competition for distinction, whether they like it or not. Most people enter it willingly. They believe they can "beat the market." Like warfare and politics, trade and investments reflect binary thinking. People distinguish between companions and ordinary people which, for an investor, means distinguishing between senior and junior investors, winners and losers, investments and divestments, "short" and "long" investments…. Investors believe that, since the market can be "beaten,"' not all have the same access to information. Some must be better connected than others. They are in a better position to influence the others and to promote their views and their projects. They have seniority over the others.

Any owner behaves as an investor when acquiring a stock with the hope that it will gain in value relative to other stocks. Any buyer hopes that the seller underestimates the value of the item and, reciprocally, the seller hopes that the buyer overestimates it. Any owner acts as a senior investor who seeks to attract more junior investors and thus increase the value of the stock more than that of competitors.

However, competition to attract junior investors can only be temporary; it can last for a long time but not forever. Indeed, there is always a limited supply of investors. Competition between investors is bound to make junior investors an ever rarer, more in-demand resource. The cost of attracting them – the return offered to them on investments – rises over time until it exceeds the benefits junior investors can bring to seniors, that is, in the most extreme case, until juniors would gain more than seniors and the positions of seniors deteriorate relative to juniors.

At that point, if not sooner, senior investors must sell their stock with the hope of triggering a general downturn in prices. This way, they can again make a larger than average benefit by "selling high." They must disinvest before junior partners can, without disclosing their intents. Business alliances come to an abrupt end.

Sooner or later even successful allies are bound to become rivals. The more a market distinguishes senior investors from junior ones, the easier the fallout and the sharper the downturn.

The breakup between senior and junior investors can be illustrated by events during the 2007–2008 stock decline. Investors reported that JP Morgan Chase, an investment bank, had offered to lend them funds if they invested in two hedge funds that were managed by the famous Mr. Madoff. The bank itself had invested into the hedge funds as a way to reduce the

250

risk for the investors and, therefore, indirectly, for itself. This collateral investment was decisive for the investors approached by the bank. One investor testified that, for him the investment bank's notes were "the final imprimatur of [the fund's] financial soundness." [3]

In early autumn 2008, the investment bank decided that Mr. Madoff's funds could represent an underestimated risk. It withdrew its own investment without notifying its clients. When the investors were informed the Madoff funds had lost most of their value, they were all the more furious that the investment bank reported no loss related to the Madoff funds.

The bank's clients who had invested with Madoff were on average relatively lucky though, and relatively senior nonetheless. Most junior investors were indeed heavy borrowers, unable to reimburse their loans except if their lenders accepted to new conditions.

In 2006-2007, a large part of the US mortgage industry dealt with such risks under codename "subprimes." At some point, most banks simply refused to "repackage" subprime loans as they had done regularly until then, prompting millions of individual defaults. Most lost their homes in the process.

A market organizes itself on the conditions of its downturns. It creates unequal access to capital and information and reduces relative gains made by seniors until they will be induced to severe ties with junior investors, which precipitates the price downturn.

Frequent upturns and downturns are a constant feature in market activity. An excellent example is the Standard and Poor's 500 index showing yearly variations in the twentieth and early twenty-first centuries. The index reflects the stock value of five-hundred large companies listed on stock exchanges in the United States. Variations are calculated between close values at the end of the year (*Figure 23*).[4]

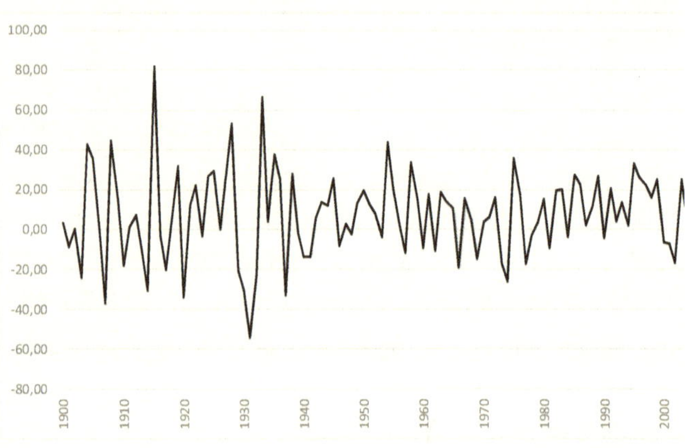

Figure 23. Market prices: SP500 index yearly variations (%), 1900-2011.

*

Ben Bernanke, former chairman of the US Federal Reserve, once referred to the explanation of the 1929 stock market crash as the "Holy Grail" of macro-economics.[5] He meant that the event was the single greatest problem in that field.

It certainly was a problem if the hypothesis was that investors were egoistic "utility-maximizers". Such actors should never have destroyed their own wealth. But changing only slightly the basic hypothesis changes everything in that respect. Let us assume that instead of utility-maximizers, investors are position-maximizers. Under a position-maximizing hypothesis, an investor's position is increased when a majority of competitors gain less or lose more than they do. There can be no individual preferences. All the decisions of investors and traders are connected. They influence one another.

As we just saw, such a hypothesis would be sufficient to explain why some investors must at some point bet "against the market" and trigger a downturn. From the greatest problem, the 1929 crash becomes a normal event.

A relationship and the exchanges it involves must seem advantageous to both sides; each one must believe they benefit from it. They must feel better off compared to the situation they would have known had there been no exchange, compared to peers who have not been parties to the exchange. Exchanges create new bonds and companionship, either in business, politics or warfare.

But the people who exchange with one another must in the long term become rivals in the competition for distinction. No one can put up with allies that indefinitely succeed as well if not better than oneself. Alliances are necessary but none can last forever. The competition between companions must periodically rekindle conflicts.

In the long term, all alliances and rivalries must align with the general bipolarization; trade and investments follow and are redirected accordingly. But when the general bipolarization stops and reverses, personal rivalries take over again; former alliances break down and new ones are made. A new bipolarization begins.

Key Takeaways

1. *The unifying theory*

This book unveils a groundbreaking scientific discovery. It presents the solution to the most complex problem ever faced by science. It marks the end of a three-hundred-year quest pursued by generations of researchers in many fields. It is the unifying theory that allows all their works to be bridged. It is a paradigm shift in the way we understand the mind and our human world.

2. *The Law of History*

A single simple algorithm ultimately commands all our thoughts and actions. It explains all events in our human world. It is the Law of History.

The human mind always obeys the same basic program because the information it receives shapes it. Although the events it perceives might seem almost infinitely varied, the mind always extracts the same basic information, regardless of the specifics. It thus acquires a simple, universal structure.

3.   *The universal structure of the mind*

No one is fully conscious of the way their mind operates, even if they think they are. They only perceive what their mind gives them. Each one is spontaneously driven to think they live in unique circumstances. They tend to ignore the conspicuous facts that prove the contrary.

The discovery of the universal structure of the mind is the result of the deep knowledge of human history that scientists have acquired over the last few centuries. The exploration of ancient and distant civilizations has increasingly revealed universal and permanent facts that could be explained by no particular national culture, language or circumstances, but required a global explanation.

4.   *To be the Hero of History*

The universal structure of the mind has all-permeating effects on our lives and on our human world. First, the stories that we create and repeat all possess the same structure. They are all alike in some respect, something we are quite aware of regarding fairy tales, but much less regarding historical accounts.

Our narratives reveal that the logic of the mind is binary. People always imagine two sides. Plus, they believe that they have an autonomous will and, every time something happens to them, they imagine wills at work, wills similar to their own. As a result, they interpret all events in the light of a heroic scenario—good versus evil—and they think of themselves as the Hero opposed to the evil Enemy.

The mind interprets all events in the same fundamental way; all convey the heroic scenario. This is why each one spontaneously develops the same basic worldview. They imagine one reality, one world and one history only; this is the condition to be the unique Hero of History, the one who will eventually destroy the unique Enemy that each one believes they know intimately, better than anyone else. No one would accept that someone else was the Hero. This is why there is no Hero in historical accounts, when one always expects one in fiction.

5.   *The need for companions*

People intimately sense the presence of the Enemy. Yet he is never met. But the mind has a way around that difficulty. It imagines that the Enemy wants to hide, the better to manipulate its victims. That idea can never be proved wrong.

The only possibility to break the Enemy's hold is to share one's intimate knowledge of him with companions; to reveal it cannot be the Enemy's plan, for he wants to stay hidden. To have companions is the first step to fight the Enemy.

Each one needs the support of companions. They cannot live without them. They are utterly dependent on them. They would turn against themselves otherwise. People must trust their companions. They accept only what their companions confirm and reject what their companions condemn.

For the sake of their companions, people not only learn to deny being the Hero. They repress the idea. Adults are perfectly convinced they do not even desire a heroic role, that they are perfectly reasonable people. They have learned to repress the idea during the adolescence. Children neither repress nor hide the idea. They have not yet discovered how hostile their friends are to it.

Adults are convinced not to nurture a desire to be the Hero. However, their mind still has the same structure as when they were children. And the repression is, after all, only the result of that same fundamental program that all must obey, even unknowingly. Becoming the Hero of History is the supreme desire. It endures in everything people think and do, even if they are not aware of it.

6. *Political animals*

All humans must interact; they all interact in a similar way, which generates a universal dynamics in human activities. Events can thus be predicted or reconstructed.

As they find companions, humans also make adversaries. Any friend implies a foe. The bipolar nature of all our interactions is the most conspicuous aspect of the universal dynamics in human interactions.

All humans constantly build alliances, and these alliances are always bipolar. One side builds up in reaction to the other. The more they interact, the more each one can recognize good and evil, and the more easily both sides attract followers. Alliances and conflicts grow until they end with the victory of one side and the defeat of the other. And these events are immediately followed by a new period of bipolarization.

7. *From rivalries to world wars*

People do not become more peaceful. In places like Europe, personal rivalries and tribal feuds have been incrementally replaced over the last millennium by international conflicts and world wars. Long-term interaction resulted in more synchronized actions.

8. *The synchronization of all human activities*

The prime driver of economics is also conflict. Although we spontaneously tend to oppose economics and war, both are inextricably linked. Economic cycles tend to synchronize with conflict cycles. Even redistribution and equality are primarily driven by the dynamics of alliance and conflicts. The more people feel the need for allies, and the more they are ready to accept equality.

Alliances, conflicts, production, redistribution, trade all tend to vary together. All human activities are cyclical. They all tend synchronize on the long term.

9.   *The illusion of reason*

Humans are social and political animals. They are not reasonable. They do not converge on a peaceful and rational government of the world. But they believe they are. And they believe that their fellow beings should be reasonable too. It enrages them to discover how prone to upsetting the natural order of the world the others really are. Their belief in reason only fuels new conflicts.

10. *Facts that everyone can observe*

This book is based on facts that everyone can observe: the capacity of the mind to make the most surprising associations of ideas, the elements that all stories share regardless of the culture, nation or time that produced them, the bipolar dynamics of all alliances and conflicts throughout history, the synchronization of all human activities…. They all point to one explanation, and one only. There is only one *Law of History*.

To be continued…

In the second Volume of *The Law of History*:

The Destiny of Civilization.

In this volume, we have uncovered the fundamental logic of the human mind and its most direct consequences.

We have found out how it makes all people imagine their world in similar terms, why we can observe a universal worldview in the structure of narratives. We have also understood how this irrepressible comprehension of the events generates constant interactions and triggers bipolarization, a universal dynamics that indices all human activities to synchronize.

In the next volume we will discover how these dynamics operate in the longer term to produce a global dynamics, civilization.

The rise and fall of civilization ultimately depends on the fundamental logic of the human mind: on the intimate, even unconscious, but supreme desire nurtured by each one of us, to be the Hero of History.

The discovery of the Law of History makes us enter a new era, where our past can be reconstructed and our future predicted.

Lexicon

Anticipation: an idea interpreted as a future experience

Bipolarization (or bipolar mobilization): acceleration and generalization in the mobilization of two (and only two) self-aware opposed coalitions together with the elaboration and growing explicitation of converging visions of history

Coalition: process of association and mutual recognition of companions and allies, always in a bipolar mobilization. Syn. *alliance*

Companion: person with whom a special relationship is established, fellowship. Companions distinguish each other from ordinary people. They can become rivals. Cf. *inherent instability*

Convergence: the production of a new history by opposed coalitions; alignment of justifications, programs and actions

Cycle: non-linear process marked by a peak (maximum) and a trough (minimum); a cycle is usually composed of cycles of lesser length and amplitude and is likewise a component of a longer cycle; successive cycles are therefore usually not of the same length and amplitude

Desire: an idea, considered as a potential of action

Distinction: result of the dissociation from ordinary people or former companions and of the association with new companions; higher social position

Enemy (The): fundamental notion. The person, the source of evil, whose destruction will forever restore peace and happiness

Exchange: any social contact, possibly accompanied by exchanges of favors or goods, vector of distinction. Cf. *companion*

Fear: a negative desire. Cf. *desire, idea*

Fellowship: the relation proper to companions

Fiction: narrative about events that are not meant to happen in reality. Ant. *historical account*

Fundamental notion: idea that is a necessary part of the universal, unconscious structure of the mind. Cf. *heroic scenario*

Fundamental sequence: simplest and most frequent information conveyed to the mind by perceptions; source of the universal structure of the mind

Hero (The): fundamental notion. The person called to destroy the Enemy. There is only one possible Hero, like there is only one Enemy. Everyone is above all attracted by the idea that one is the Hero, but represses the idea as no companion would ever confirm it

Heroic scenario: combination of the fundamental notions. Each one sees themselves as the Hero of History, the one called to defeat the Enemy and to restore the universal peace

Historical account: narrative pertaining to real events. Ant. *fiction*

History (The): fundamental notion. All the real events happening in our world

Idea: generic psychic event, consequence of an association of ideas, cause of associations of ideas, source of actions. Notions, desires, fears, memories are ideas considered through specific effects

Inherent instability: property of fellowship due to ambiguity of feelings, source of bipolar rivalries and conflicts

International society: national coalitions in interaction, either allied or opposed

Madness: universal notion. The state of being governed by the Enemy, of not understanding the true nature of things. Ant. *Reason*

Memory: an idea interpreted as a past experience

Mind: the general process of association of ideas, including perceptions

Mobilization: the disinvestment of day-dreaming and the investment of interactions; fuels the acceleration of the bipolarization; positively correlated to production, redistribution, trade and innovation

Nation: imagined community regrouping many families and preceding them historically; nationals share common ancestors

Notion: an idea conceived unawares. Cf. *idea*

Ordinary people: universal notion. Normal people, distinct from companions. They do not suspect of the presence of the Enemy and do his biddings. Materialist, egoist people

Perceptions: ideas generated by sensory messages

Pull: attractiveness of an idea, proportional to the exposure to similar information

Quest for heroism: the desire to be the Hero of History; actions undertaken to fulfill that destiny

Reason: universal notion. The capacity to rule harmoniously, based on the understanding of the true nature of things. Ant. *Madness.*

Sensory message: influx produced by stimulation of a sense, cause of a perception

Spontaneously: by itself, without external cause

Structure: a permanent feature or property, as opposed to variable ones, in a series of objects or in a changing object

System: a stable whole, the components of which interact harmoniously, performing stable functions or adjusting to maintain the whole stable

Tale: the type of fiction that reflects most directly the heroic scenario; the most easily distinguished from reality

World (The): fundamental notion. The universe in which all actions take place. Coroll. Enemy, Hero and History (There can be only one World and one History if there is only one Enemy and one Hero)

Illustrations

Index

Bibliography

Anderson, B. (1991). *Imagined communities* (2 ed.). London: Verso.

Arendt, H. (1972). *Crises of the republic.* New York: Harcourt.

Aristotle. (c.-335/1898). *Poetics* (2nd ed.). (S. H. Butcher, Trans.) London: Macmillan.

Barrinuevo, A. (2011, October 12). A year out of the dark in Chile, but still trapped. *The New York Times.*

Barthes, R. (1966/1975). An introduction to the structural analysis of narrative. (L. Duisit, Trans.). *New Literary History, 6*(2), 237-272. doi: 10.2307/468419.

Beck, A. T. (2000). *Prisoners of hate. The cognitive basis of anger, hostility and violence.* New York: Harper.

Benassi, D. (2010). 'Father of the welfare state'? Beveridge and the emergence of the welfare state. *Sociologica, 3*, 1-20.

Bernanke, B. S. (1995). The macroeconomics of the great depression: a comparative approach. *Journal of Money, Credit and Banking, 27*(1).

Beveridge, W. (1942). *Social insurance and allied services, report to the Parliament.* London: His Majesty's Stationery Services.

Bilderberg: Alex Jones disrupts BBC's sunday politics. (2013, June 9). Retrieved from BBC News UK: http://www.bbc.com/news/uk-22832994.

Bilefsky, D. (2009, November 18). Celebrating revolution with roots in a rumor. *The New York Times.*

Bourgoin, N. (1993). Le suicide en milieu carcéral [Suicide in prison]. *Population, 48*(3), 609-625.

Brémond, C. (1966/1980). The logic of narrative possibilities. (E.D. Cancalon Trans.). *New Literary History, 11*, 387-411. doi: 10.2307/468934.

Brosnan, S. F., & De Waal, F. B. (2003). Monkeys reject unequal pay. *Nature, 425*, 297-299.

Campbell, J. (1949/2008). *The hero with a thousand faces.* Novato: New World Library.

Carré de Malberg, R. (1920/1985). *Théorie générale de l'état [General theory of the state].* Paris: Editions du CNRS.

Cervantes Saavedra, M. d. (1605/1853). *Don Quixote de la Mancha.* London: Henry Bohn.

Chivers, C. J. (2011, September 15). Top medal for marine who saved many lives. *The New York Times.*

Chomsky, N. (1969). *Aspects of the theory of syntax* (2 ed.). Cambridge, MA: The MIT Press.

Chrétien de Troyes. (c. 1200/1997). *Lancelot: the knight of the cart.* (B. Raffel , Trans.) New Haven: Yale University Press.

Cikara, M., Botvinick, M. M., & Fiske, S. T. (2011). Us versus them. Social identity shapes neural responses to intergroup competition and harm. *Psychological Science, 22*(3), 306-313. doi:10.1177/0956797610397667.

Citron, S. (1989). *Le mythe national: L'histoire de France en question [The national myth: questioning the history of France].* Paris: Les Editions ouvrières.

Clausewitz, C. v. (1832/1989). On war. In M. Howard, & P. Paret (Eds.), *On war* (M. Howard, & P. Paret, Trans., pp. 61-714). Princeton, NJ: Princeton University Press.

Copernicus, N. (1543/1995). *On the revolutions of heavenly spheres.* New York: Prometheus Books.

Crichton, M. (2006). *Timeline.* London: Arrow Books.

Dagett, S., & Belasco, A. (2002). *Defense budget for FY2003. Data summary.* Washington DC: Congressional Research Service.

Darwin, C. (1859/1998). *The origin of species.* London: Wordsworth.

Dehaene-Lambertz, G., & Dehaene, S. (1994). Speed and cerebral correlates of syllable discrimination in infants. *Nature, 370*(6487), 292–295.

Diener, E., Wirtz, D., & Shigehiro, O. (2001). End effects of rated life quality. the James Dean effect. *Psychological Science*(12), 124-128.

Eco, U. (1984). *The role of the reader. Explorations in the semiotics of texts.* Bloomington: Indiana University Press.

Eco, U. (1998). *Serendipities. Language and lunacy.* New York: Columbia University Press.

Einstein, A. (1920). *Relativity. The special and the general theory. A popular exposition.* London: Methuen.

Elias, N. (1939/2000). *The civilizing process.* Oxford: Blackwell.

Emde, R. N. (1983). The prerepresentational self and its affective core. *The Psychoanalytic Study of the Child*(38), 163-192.

Emmerich, R. (Director). (2000). *The patriot* [Motion Picture]. United States: Columbia Pictures.

Fellman, M. (2011, November 9). Sherman's demons. *The New York Times.*

Fraisse, P. (1994). *La psychologie expérimentale [Experimental psychology].* Paris: Presses universitaires de France.

Freine (de), S. (1965). *The great silence.* Dublin: Foilseacháin Náisiúnta Teoranta.

Freud, S. (1908/1968). Family romances. In S. Freud, *The complete psychological works (1906-1908)* (Vol. IX, pp. 236-241). London: The Hogarth Press.

Freud, S. (1917/1989). *Introductory lectures on psycho-analysis.* New York: Norton.

Freud, S. (1939/2010). *Moses and monotheism.* Mansfield, CT: Martino.

Fukuyama, F. (1992/1998). *The end of history and the last man.* New York: Avon.

Gatti, C., & Henriques, D. B. (2009, January 29). JPMorgan exited Madoff-linked funds last fall. *The New York Times.*

Gauthier & Deschamps. (1904). *Histoire de France, cours élémentaire.* Paris: Armand Collin.

Gawronski, B., Walther, E., & Blank, H. (2005). Cognitive consistency and the formation of interpersonal attitudes. Cognitive balance affects the encoding of social information. *Journal of Experimental Social Psychology*, 618-626.

Gellner, E. (1983/2006). *Nations and nationalism.* Ithaca, NY: Cornell University Press.

Gewen, B. (2014, September 1). Rebels who had a cause. Havel and Michnik after communism. *The New York Times.*

Gick, B., & Derrick, D. (2009). Aero-tactile integration in speech perception. *Nature*(462), 502-4.

Giddens, A. (1979). *Central problems in social theory. Action, structure and contradiction in social science.* Berkeley: University of California Press.

Girodet-Trioson, A.-L. (1801). *Ossian receiving the ghosts of the fallen French heroes.* [Oil on canvas. 192 cm x 182 cm]. Rueil-Malmaison: Musée National de Malmaison.

Goethe, J. W. (1808/2008). *Faust. Eine Tragödie [Faust. A tragedy]*. Münster: Aschendorff.

Goldstein, J. (1987). Long waves in war, production, prices and wage. New empirical evidence. *The Journal of Conflict Resolution, 31*(4), 573-600.

Goldstein, J. (1988). *Long cycles. Prosperity and war in the modern age.* London and New Haven: Yale University Press.

Grimm, J., & Grimm, W. (1816/2010). *The complete Grimm's fairy tales.* Seven Treasures.

Grosjean, B., & Méron, M. (2014, March 20). Barbara, contaminée par son compagnon : vingt ans de sida et de colère [Barbara, contaminated by her partner: twenty years with AIDS and anger]. *Rue 89.*

Grossman, S., & Stieglitz, J. (1980). On the impossibility of informationally efficient markets. *American Economic Review, 70*(3), 393-408.

Gwartney, J. (2003). *Economics.* Mason: Thomson South Western.

Hadjikhani, N., Kveraga, K., & Paulami, N. (2009). Early (N170) activation of face-specific cortex by face-like objects. *Neuroreport, 20*(4), 403–407. doi:10.1097/WNR.0b013e328325a8e1.

Hall, P. A., & Taylor, R. C. (1996). *Political science and the three new institutionalisms.* Paper presented to the MPIFG Scientific Advisory Board, 9 May.

Hamilton, G. (Director). (1969). *Battle of Britain* [Motion Picture]. United Kingdom: Metro Goldwyn Meyer.

Hamlin, K. J., Wynn, K., & Bloom, P. (2007). Social evaluation by preverbal infants. *Nature, 450,* 557-559. doi: 10.1038/nature06288.

Hand, D. (Director). (1937). *Snow White and the seven dwarfs* [Motion Picture]. United States of America: Walt Disney - RKO.

Hanson, C. (Director). (1997). *LA confidential* [Motion Picture]. United States of America: Warner.

Harris, L. T., & Fiske, S. T. (2011). Dehumanized perception. A psychological means to facilitate atrocities, torture, and genocide? *Zeitschrift fur Psychologie, 219*(3), 175-181. doi:10.1027/2151-2604/a000065.

Hayes, A. (2019, June 25). *Perfect competition.* Retrieved from Investopedia: https://www.investopedia.com/

Hobbes, T. (1651/1929). Leviathan or the matter, forme & power of a common-wealth ecclesiastical & civill. In W. G. Pogson-

Smith (Ed.), *Hobbes's Leviathan* (2nd ed., pp. 9-557). Oxford: Oxford University Press.

Hobsbawm, E. (1990). *Nations and nationalism since 1780. Programme, myth, reality*. Cambridge: Cambridge University Press.

Hobster, J. R. (1988). *Amadis de Gaula in Don Quijote*. Durham: Durham theses, Durham University.

Hofer, M. A. (1987). Early social relationships. A pyschobiologist's view. *Child Development, 58*(3), 633-647.

Hume, D. (1739/1888). A treatise of human nature. Being an attempt to introduce the experimental method of reasoning into moral subjects. Book I. Of the understanding. In L. A. Selby-Bigge (Ed.), *Hume's treastise of human nature* (pp. xix-709). Oxford: Oxford University Press.

Jackson, P. (Director). (2013). *The hobbit. The desolation of Smaug* [Motion Picture]. New Zealand: Warner.

Jacobs, E. P. (1953/2006). *The secret of the swordfish*. Paris: Blake & Mortimer.

Jefferys, K. (1994). *War and reform. British politics during the Second World War*. Manchester: Manchester University Press.

Kahneman, D. (2012). *Thinking fast and slow*. London: Random House.

Kant, I. (1781/1992). *Theoretical philosophy, 1755–1770*. (D. Walford, & R. Meerbote, Trans.) Cambridge: Cambridge University Press.

Kelsen, H. (1960). *Pure theory of law* (2 ed.). Berkeley: University of California Press.

Kershner, I. (Director). (1980). *Star wars episode V. The empire strikes back* [Motion Picture]. United States of America: 20th Century Fox.

Keynes, J. M. (1936/2007). *The general theory of employment, interest and money*. London: Macmillan.

Kondratieff, N. D. (1926/1935). The long waves in economic life. *Review of Economic Statistics, 17*, 105-115.

Konvalinka, I.; Xygalatas, D.; Bulbulia, J.; Schjødt, U.; Jegindø, E.-M., Wallot, S.,... Roepstorff, A. (2011). Synchronized arousal between performers and related spectators in a fire-walking ritual. *Proceedings of the National Academy of Sciences, 108*, 8514-8519. doi: 10.1073/pnas.1016955108.

Kovács, A. M., Téglás, E., & Endress, A. D. (2010). The social sense. Susceptibility to others' beliefs in human infants and adults. *Science, 330*, 1830-1834. doi: 10.1126/science.1190792.

Krugman, P. (1980). Scale economies, product differenciation and the pattern of trade. *The American Economic Review, 70*(5), 950-959.

Krugman, P. (2012, December 4). Asimov's Foundation novels grounded my economics. *The Guardian*.

Kuhn, T. (1970/1996). *The structure of scientific revolutions* (2nd ed.). Chicago: Chicago University Press.

Kuklinski, J. H. (2002). *Thinking about political psychology*. Cambridge: Cambridge University Press.

Kwan, V. S., & Fiske, S. T. (2008). Missing links in social cognition: The continuum from nonhuman agents to dehumanized humans. *Social Cognition, 26*(2), 125–128. doi.org/10.1521/soco.2008.26.2.125.

Landau, M., Sullivan, D., & Greenberg, J. (2009). Evidence that self-relevant motives and metaphoric framing interact to influence political and social attitudes. *Psychological Science, 20*, 1421-1427. doi: 10.1111/j.1467-9280.2009.02462.x.

Lang, A. (1898/1997). *Arabian nights, after the book of the thousand nights and a night by Richard F. Burton, 1885*. London: Penguin Books.

L'assassinat de l'Archiduc Franz Ferdinand. (1914, July 12). *Le Petit Journal*.

Latour, B. (1988). *The pasteurization of France*. Cambridge, MA: Harvard University Press.

Lavisse , E. (1913). *Histoire de France. Cours élémentaire [History of France. Elementary curriculum]*. Paris: Armand Collin.

Leca, J. (2001). Le politique comme fondation [Politics as a foundation]. *EspacesTemps*(76-77), 27-36.

Lévi-Strauss, C. (1964/1975). *The raw and the cooked. Introduction to a science of mythology* (Vol. I). New York: Harper.

Lewis, T., Amini, F., & Lannon, R. (2001). *A general theory of love*. New York: Random House.

Libet, B. (1985). Unconscious, cerebral initiative and the role of conscious will in voluntary action. *Behavioural and Brain Sciences, 8*(4), 529-566. doi: 10.1017/S0140525X00044903.

Locke, J. (1690/1929). *An essay concerning human understanding* (25th ed.). London: Tegg.

Lommen, M. J., Engelhard, I. M., & Hout, M. (2013). Susceptibility to long-term misinformation effect outside of the laboratory. *European Journal of Psychotraumatology, 4*, 1-7. http://dx.doi.org/10.3402/ejpt.v4i0.19864.

Lucas, G. (Director). (1977). *Star wars episode IV. A new hope* [Motion Picture]. United States of America.

Lucas, G. (Director). (1999). *Star wars episode I. The phantom menace* [Motion Picture]. United States of America: 20th Century Fox.

Mackay, R. (1999). *The test of war: inside Britain 1939-1945.* London: University College London.

Mackey, R. (2014, October 14). Soccer match in Serbia erupts in riot set off by drone. *The New York Times.*

Malot, H. (1878/2012). *Nobody's boy.* CreateSpace Independent Publishing Platform.

Mandelbaum, E. (2016). Attitude, inference, association. On the propositional structure of implicit bias. *Noûs, 50*(3), 629-658.

Marquand, R. (Director). (1983). *Star wars episode VI. Return of the jedi* [Motion Picture]. United States of America: 20th Century Fox.

Marsh, J. (Director). (2014). *The theory of everything* [Motion Picture]. United States: Universal Pictures.

Massie, R. K. (1992). *Dreadnought. Britain, Germany, and the coming of the Great War.* New York: Ballantine Books.

Mauss, M. (1924/2011). *The gift, forms and functions of exchange in archaic societies.* Mansfield: Martino.

Michelis, C. G. (2004). *The non-existent manuscript: A study of the protocols of the Sages of Zion.* Lincoln: University of Nebraska Press.

Michnik, A. (2014). *The trouble with history. Morality, revolution, and counterrevolution.* New Haven: Yale University Press.

Morin, E. (1973). *Le paradigme perdu. La nature humaine [The lost paradigm. Human nature].* Paris: Sueil.

Nash, J. (1950). The bargaining problem. *Econometrica, 18*(2), 155-162.

Newton, I. (1687). *Philosophiæ naturalis principia mathematica.* London: Streater, Joseph.

Nicolson, A. (2006). *Men of honor. Trafalgar and the making of the English hero.* London: Harper Perennial.

Oi, M. (2013, March 14). *What Japanese history lessons leave out.* Retrieved from BBC News Tokyo: http://www.bbc.co.uk

Olson, M. (1965/1971). *The logic of collective action* (2nd ed.). Cambridge: Harvard University Press.

Oswald, A., & Zizzo, D. J. (2000). *Are people willing to pay to reduce others' income ?* Retrieved January 22, 2003, from http://www.warwick.ac.uk

Pavlov, I. (1906). The scientific investigation of the psychical faculties or processes in the higher animals. *Science, 24*(620), 613-619.

Perrault, C. (1697/1993). *The complete fairy tales.* New York: Clarion.

Petersen, W. (Director). (2001). *The perfect storm* [Motion Picture]. United States of America: Warner.

Picketty, T., & Saez, E. (2003). Income inequality in the United States, 1913-1998. *The Quarterly Journal of Economics, 118*(1), 1-39.

Piela, R. (1996). Frei nach Heinrich Hoffmann [Freely after Heinrich Hoffmann]. *Zweisprachigkeit, 12*, p. 8.

Plutarch. (c. 120/2009). *Lives.* Digireads.com.

Pronin, E. (2008). How we see ourselves and how we see others. *Science, 320*, 1177-1180. doi: 10.1126/science.1154199.

Propp, V. (1928/2009). *Morphology of the folktale.* Austin: University of Texas Press.

Quammen, D. (2018, August 13). The scientist who scrambled Darwin's tree of life. *The New York Times.*

Rank, O. (1922/2004). The myth of the birth of the hero. In R. A. Segal (Ed.), *The myth of the birth of the hero. A psychological exploration of myth* (G. C. Richter, & J. E. Liebermann, Trans., pp. 1-127). Baltimore: Johns Hopkins University Press.

Reid, J. (1990). Cover artwork. In Anhrefn, *Dragon's revenge.* Llandwrog-Caernarfon: Canolfan Sain.

Riagain, P. O., & Gliasain, M. O. (1979). *All-Irish primary schools in the Dublin area.* Dublin: Instituid Teangeolaiochta Eireann.

Ricoeur, P., Collins, F., & Perron, P. (1989). Greimas's narrative grammar. *New Literary History, 20*, 581-608. doi:10.2307/469355.

Rokeach, M. (1964). *The three Christs of Ypsilanti,.* New York: Alfred A. Knopf.

Rosenbaum, R. A. (2010). *Waking to danger. Americans and Nazi Germany, 1933-1941.* Santa Barbara: Greenwood Press.

Rosselini, R. (Director). (1950). *Stromboli* [Motion Picture]. Italy: RKO.

Rouget de Lisle, C. J. (1792/2009). *Le chant de guerre pour l'armée du Rhin, dit la Marseillaise.* Retrieved March 05, 2009, from Assemblée Nationale: http://www.assemblee-nat.fr

Rousseau, J.-J. (1762/1968). *The social contract.* London: Penguin.

Rowling, J. K. (2007). *Harry Potter and the deathly hallows.* London: Bloomsbury.

Sabatier, P. A. (1999). *Theories of the policy process.* Boulder: Westview Press.

Scheidhauer, C. (2004). *La convergence européenne des politiques de promotion de l'enseignement des langues régionales, fruit de la quête d'héroïsme des promoteurs [European convergence of policies promoting regional language teaching, due to the promoter's quest for heroism].* Doctoral thesis, Institut d'Etudes Politique, Paris.

Schelling, T. (1960/2006). *The strategy of conflict.* Cambridge: Harvard University Press.

Schmidt, R. (2000). *Language policy and identity politics in the United States.* Philadelphia: Temple University Press.

Scott, W. (1820/1994). *Ivanhoe.* London: Penguin.

Sechrist, G., & Stangor, C. (2001). Perceived consensus influences intergroup behavior and stereotype accessibility. *Journal of Personality and Social Psychology, 80*(4), pp. 645-654. Retrieved from http://psycnet.apa.org/journals/psp/80/4/645/

Seligman, M. E., & Maier, S. F. (1967). Failure to escape traumatic shock. *Journal of Experimental Psychology, 74*(1), 1-9. doi: http://dx.doi.org/10.1037/h0024514.

Shakespeare, W. (1584/1998). *Hamlet.* Oxford: Oxford University Press.

Shakespeare, W. (1599/1994). *Henry V.* London: Penguin Books.

Sherif, M., Harvey, O. J., White, B. J., Hood, W. R., & Sherif, C. V. (1961/1988). *The robbers cave experiment. Intergroup conflict and cooperation.* Middletown, CT: Wesleyan University Press.

Smith, A. D. (1999). *Myths and memories of the nations.* Oxford: Oxford University Press.

Spitz, R. (1945). Hospitalism: an inquiry into the genesis of psychiatric conditions in early childhood. *Psychoanalysis Study of the Child*(I), 53-74.

Stahl, A., & Feigenson, L. (2015). Cognitive development. Observing the unexpected enhances infants' learning and exploration. *Science, 348*, 91-4. doi:10.1126/science.aaa3799

Standard&Poor's. (2021, 05 04). *S&P 500 historical annual returns.* Retrieved 05 04, 2021, from Macrotrends: https://www.macrotrends.net

Supreme Court of the United States. (2014). *The court and constitutional interpretation.* Retrieved November 24, 2014, from The Supreme Court of the United States: http://www.supremecourt.gov

Titian (Tiziano Vecellio). (1533). *Portrait of Alfonso d'Avalos, Marquis of Vasto.* [Oil on canvas, 1,10 m x 0,80 m]. Los Angeles: The J. Paul Getty Museum.

Titian (Tiziano Vecellio). (1548). *Portrait of Charles V seated.* [Oil on canvas, 2,03 m x 1,22 m]. Munich: Alte Pinakothek.

Tolkien, J. R. (1937/2011). *The hobbit or there and back again.* London: Harper Collins.

Tolkien, J. R. (1954/2004). *The lord of the rings.* New York: HMH.

Trye Maison (de), G. (1911). *Illustration for a advertising campaign by Anios Laboratories and Pasteur Institute.* Paris: Institut Pasteur.

U.S. Bureau for economic analysis. (2010). *Gross domestic product, percent change from preceding period.* Retrieved November 3, 2010, from http://www.bea.gov

Uccello, P. (1515). Saint George slaying the dragon. In A. Barclay, *Life of Saint George.* Westminster: Anonymous Publisher.

United Nations Organization. (1945/2014). *Charter of the United Nations.* Retrieved November 24, 2014, from UNO: http://www.un.org

United States of America. (2014). *The constitution.* Retrieved November 24, 2014, from The White House: http://www.whitehouse.gov

Valdes, A. L. (2004, December 16). Des trolls, des mariages virtuels... et une vraie guerre [Trolls, virtual weddings... and a real war]. *Courrier international, 767.*

Vernes, J. (1870/2006). *20,000 leagues under the sea.* New York: Sterling.

Vickhoff, B., Malmgren, H., Åström, R., Nyberg, G., Ekström, S. R., Engwall, M., & et al. (2013). Music structure determines heart rate variability of singers. *Frontier Psychology, 334*(4), 1-16.

Weber, M. (1946). *Essays in sociology.* New York: Oxford University Press.

Weir, P. (Director). (2003). *Master and commander. The far side of the world* [Motion Picture]. United States of America: 20th Century Fox.

West, B. (1806). *The death of Nelson.* [Oil on canvas, 182.5 cm × 247.5 cm]. Liverpool: Walker Art Gallery.

Whishaw, B., & Kolb, I. Q. (2010). *An introduction to brain and behavior* (3rd ed.). New York: Worth Publishers.

Wickham, C. (2009). *The inheritance of Rome.* London: Penguin.

Widmer, T. (2011, February 21). All or nothing. *The New York Times.*

Williams, L. E., & Bargh, J. A. (2008). Experiencing physical warmth promotes interpersonal warmth. *Science, 322*(5901), 606-607.

Notes

The Revolution of Human Science

1. Hume, 1739/1888, p. xx
2. Kuhn, 1970/1996, p. 10
3. Kuhn, 1970/1996, p. 136
4. Kuhn, 1970/1996, p. 2
5. Kuhn, 1970/1996, p. ix
6. Goethe, 1808/2008, p. 24
7. Marsh, 2014
8. Kuhn, 1970/1996, pp. ix, 6, 48, 52
9. Kuhn, 1970/1996, p. 155
10. Copernicus, 1543/1995
11. Quammen, 2018
12. Locke, 1690/1825, p. 4
13. Hume, 1739/1888, pp. 30, 209; 234
14. Kant, 1781/1992, p. 387
15. Giddens, 1979, pp. 2, 50
16. Newton, 1687
17. Einstein, 1920
18. Darwin, 1859/1998
19. Krugman, 2012
20. Morin, 1973
21. Rank, 1922/2004, p. 2
22. Barthes, 1966/1975, p. 238
23. Lévi-Strauss, 1964/1975, pp. 1, 5, 11, 26
24. Rank, 1922/2004, pp. 2-3
25. Kondratiev, 1926/1935, p. 111
26. Goldstein, 1987, p. 573
27. Kondratiev, 1926/1935
28. Chomsky, 1969

I. The Logic of the Mind

1. An Autonomous Universe

1. Whishaw & Kolb, 2010, p. 72
2. Locke, 1690/1929, p. 283
3. Fraisse, 1994, p. 32
4. Gick & Derrick, 2009, pp. 502-504
5. Williams & Bargh, 2008, pp. 606-607
6. Landau, Sullivan, & Greenberg, 2009, pp. 1421-1427

2. A Spontaneous Logic

1. Pavlov, 1906, pp. 613-617
2. Dehaene-Lambertz & Dehaene, 1994, p. 293
3. Stahl & Feigenson, 2015, p. 91

3. A Universal Drive

1. Gawronski, Walther, & Blank, 2005
2. Mandelbaum, 2016

3. Seligman & Maier, 1967, pp. 1-9
4. Libet, 1985, pp. 529, 534
5. Libet, 1985, p. 530
6. Kwan & Fiske, 2008
7. Hamlin, Wynn, & Bloom, 2007
8. Hadjikhani, Kveraga, & Paulami, 2009, p. 4
9. Diener, Wirtz, & Shigehiro, 2001
10. Kahneman, 2012, p. 387
11. Locke, 1690/1929, pp. 4, 50, 51, 283
12. Locke, 1690/1929, p. 8
13. Locke, 1690/1929, p. 14
14. Locke, 1690/1929, p. 286
15. Hume, 1739/1888, p. 7
16. Hume, 1739/1888, p. 204
17. Hume, 1739/1888, p. 259
18. Hume, 1739/1888, p. 30

4. An Unspeakable Desire

1. Rokeach, 1964

II. To Be the Hero of History

5. A Universal Scenario

1. Grimm & Grimm, 1816/2010, pp. 65-69
2. Lang, 1898/1997, pp. 100-127
3. Citron, 1989, pp. 27-41
4. Gauthier & Deschamps, 1904, p. 3
5. Freine (de), 1965, p. 1
6. Scheidhauer, 2004, pp. 388-394, 519
7. Fukuyama, 1992/1998
8. Propp, 1928/2009, p. 77
9. Propp, 1928/2009, pp. 93-99
10. Propp, 1928/2009, p. 102
11. Brémond, 1966/1980, pp. 389-392 ; Barthes, 1966/1975, p. 259
12. Ricoeur, Collins, & Perron, 1989, p. 601
13. Campbell, 1949/2008, p. 23
14. Rank, 1922/2004, pp. 2-3
15. Lévi-Strauss, 1964/1975, pp. 1, 5, 11, 26
16. Barthes, 1966/1975, p. 272
17. Aristotle, c.-335/1898, p. 89
18. Barthes, 1966/1975, p. 251
19. Smith A. D., 1999, pp. 63-68

6. A Unique History

1. Tolkien, 1954/2004
2. Tolkien, 1937/2011
3. Jackson, 2013
4. Lucas, 1977
5. Lang, 1898/1997, p. 127
6. Vernes, 1870/2006
7. Lucas, 1999
8. Valdes, 2004
9. Plutarch, c. 120/2009, pp. 5-22
10. Propp, 1928/2009, p. 102
11. Perrault, 1697/1993, pp. 45-53
12. Grimm & Grimm, 1816/2010
13. Hand, 1937
14. Eco, 1984
15. Hobster, 1988
16. Cervantes Saavedra, 1605/1853
17. Scott, 1820/1994
18. Chrétien de Troyes, c. 1200/1997

7. A Unique Goal, from Childhood on

1. Freud, 1908/1968, p. 238
2. Malot, 1878/2012
3. Crichton, 2006
4. Rank, 1922/2004, pp. 385-6
5. Freud, 1939/2010, p. 23
6. Freud, 1939/2010, p. 52
7. Scheidhauer, 2004, pp. 429-430
8. Emmerich, 2000
9. Rowling, 2007
10. Lucas, 1977
11. Kershner, 1980
12. Marquand, 1983
13. Rank, 1922/2004, pp. 2-3
14. Freud, 1917/1989, pp. 256, 393, 459
15. Freud, 1908/1968, pp. 236-241
16. Freud, 1939/2010, p. 18
17. Freud, 1917/1989, p. 410
18. Freud, 1917/1989, p. 417
19. Shakespeare, 1584/1998
20. Rank, 1922/2004, p. 165

8. A Unique, Intimate Enemy

1. Petersen, 2001
2. Latour, 1988, p. 10
3. Trye Maison (de), 1911
4. Perrault, 1697/1993, pp. 82-95
5. Piela, 1996
6. Scheidhauer, 2004, pp. 366, 614
7. Scheidhauer, 2004, p. 529
8. Hanson, 1997

III. Making History

9. Revealed Truths

1. Lewis, Amini, & Lannon, 2001, pp. 68-69
2. Spitz, 1945
3. Hofer, 1987
4. Konvalinka, I.; Xygalatas, D.; Bulbulia, J.; Schjødt, U.; Jegindø, E.-M., Wallot, S.,... Roepstorff, A., 2011, p. 8515
5. Vickhoff, et al., 2013, p. 1
6. Emde, 1983
7. Lommen, Engelhard, & Hout, 2013, pp. 1-7
8. Kovács, Téglás, & Endress, 2010, pp. 1830-1834
9. Sechrist & Stangor, 2001, p. 649
10. Pronin, 2008, pp. 1177-1180
11. Konvalinka, I.; Xygalatas, D.; Bulbulia, J.; Schjødt, U.; Jegindø, E.-M., Wallot, S., et al., 2011, p. 8515
12. Harris & Fiske, 2011, pp. 175-176
13. Cikara, Botvinick, & Fiske, 2011, p. 306
14. Hamlin, Wynn, & Bloom, 2007, p. 557

10. Telling Friends from Foes

1. Nicolson, 2006, p. 151
2. Grosjean & Méron, 2014
3. Bilderberg: Alex Jones disrupts BBC's sunday politics, 2013
4. Bourgoin, 1993, p. 621
5. Fellman, 2011
6. Fellman, 2011
7. Fellman, 2011

11. Converging Hostilities

1. Michelis, 2004, pp. 76-80
2. Eco, 1998, p. 14

3. Rosenbaum, 2010, p. 41
4. Bilefsky, 2009
5. L'assassinat de l'Archiduc Franz Ferdinand, 1914
6. Mackey, 2014
7. Oi, 2013
8. Oi, 2013
9. Arendt, 1972, p. 24
10. Arendt, 1972, pp. 25-29
11. Arendt, 1972, p. 45
12. Beck, 2000, p. 163
13. Beck, 2000, p. 163
14. Beck, 2000, pp. 200-202
15. Beck, 2000, p. 163
16. Clausewitz, 1832/1989, p. 76
17. Clausewitz, 1832/1989, p. 76
18. Clausewitz, 1832/1989, pp. 75, 83
19. Clausewitz, 1832/1989, p. 88
20. Clausewitz, 1832/1989, p. 77

12. The International Bipolarization

1. Hobbes, 1651/1929, pp. 94-98
2. Goldstein, 1988, pp. 236-237
3. Goldstein, 1988, pp. 236-237
4. Sherif, Harvey, White, Hood, & Sherif, 1961/1988, pp. 58-69
5. Sherif, Harvey, White, Hood, & Sherif, 1961/1988, p. 172
6. Wickham, 2009, p. 154

13. From Personal Rivalries to World War

1. Massie, 1992, pp. 136-137
2. Massie, 1992, pp. 134-135

3. Massie, 1992, pp. 172-179
4. Massie, 1992, pp. 594-601
5. Massie, 1992, pp. 181, 184
6. Massie, 1992, p. 486
7. Massie, 1992, p. 848
8. Massie, 1992, p. 108
9. Massie, 1992, pp. 108, 138
10. Massie, 1992, pp. 106-107
11. Massie, 1992, p. 105
12. Massie, 1992, p. 151
13. Massie, 1992, pp. 166-167
14. Massie, 1992, p. 173
15. Massie, 1992, p. 166
16. Massie, 1992, p. 309
17. Massie, 1992, pp. 346, 601
18. Massie, 1992, p. 502
19. Massie, 1992, pp. 405, 530
20. Massie, 1992, p. 540
21. Massie, 1992, p. 525
22. Massie, 1992, p. 520
23. Massie, 1992, pp. 170-172
24. Massie, 1992, p. 512
25. Massie, 1992, p. 804

14. Beyond Reason & Above all Laws

1. United Nations Organization, 1945/2014
2. United States of America, 2014
3. Supreme Court of the United States, 2014
4. Widmer, 2011
5. Scheidhauer, 2004, pp. 541-544
6. Scheidhauer, 2004, pp. 572-579, 584
7. Scheidhauer, 2004, pp. 526-530, 547
8. Reid, 1990
9. Uccello, 1515

10. Schmidt, 2000
11. Gellner, 1983/2006, pp. 24, 38
12. Gellner, 1983/2006, pp. 9-10
13. Gellner, 1983/2006, pp. 41-42
14. Hobsbawm, 1990, p. 1
15. Kelsen, 1960
16. Carré de Malberg, 1920/1985, pp. 1-16
17. Weber, 1946, p. 78
18. Rousseau, 1762/1968, p. 20
19. Leca, 2001, pp. 28-36
20. Chomsky, 1969, pp. 3, 15, 25

IV. A General Mobilization

15. Distinguished Companions

1. Shakespeare, 1599/1994
2. Nicolson, 2006, p. 125
3. Hamilton, 1969
4. Merriam-Webster Online Dictionary
5. Olson, 1965/1971, p. 51
6. Anderson, 1991, p. 7
7. Hall & Taylor, 1996, pp. 17-21
8. Kuklinski, 2002, pp. 18-19
9. Schelling, 1960/2006, p. 6
10. Sabatier, 1999, p. 140
11. Gwartney, 2003, p. 6
12. Grossman & Stieglitz, 1980, p. 393 ; Keynes, 1936/2007, p. 156
13. Nash, 1950

16. Enlisting Ordinary People

1. Scheidhauer, 2004, pp. 449-455
2. Riagain & Gliasain, 1979
3. Lavisse , 1913, p. 161

4. Scheidhauer, 2004, pp. 332-337

17. A Competition to Mobilize

1. Jefferys, 1994, p. 89
2. Mackay, 1999, p. 196
3. Mackay, 1999, pp. 90, 97-98
4. Benassi, 2010, p. 7 ; Beveridge, 1942, p. 8
5. Mackay, 1999, p. 196
6. Beveridge, 1942, p. 6
7. Gewen, 2014
8. Michnik, 2014
9. Gewen, 2014
10. Barrinuevo, 2011

18. Conflits, the Drive of Economy

1. Dagett & Belasco, 2002, pp. 24-25
2. U.S. Bureau for economic analysis, 2010
3. Picketty & Saez, 2003, p. 1
4. Kondratiev, 1926/1935, pp. 24-39
5. Goldstein, 1987, pp. 582-7
6. Kondratiev, 1926/1935, p. 35
7. Kondratiev, 1926/1935, p. 42

V. The Competition for Distinction

19. Allies and Rivals

1. Weir, 2003
2. Jacobs, 1953/2006, pp. 46-54
3. Chivers, 2011
4. Rouget de Lisle, 1792/2009
5. West, 1806
6. Girodet-Trioson, 1801

20. Reciprocal Favors

1. Mauss, 1924/2011, pp. 10-11
2. Mauss, 1924/2011, p. 27
3. Mauss, 1924/2011, pp. 1, 12
4. Mauss, 1924/2011, p. 35
5. Mauss, 1924/2011, p. 11
6. Mauss, 1924/2011, p. 81
7. Elias, 1939/2000, p. 103
8. Elias, 1939/2000, p. 101
9. Elias, 1939/2000, p. 104
10. Rosselini, 1950

21. To Prove One's Worth

1. Merriam Webster Online Dictionary
2. Mauss, 1924/2011, p. 20
3. Mauss, 1924/2011, p. 36
4. Titian (Tiziano Vecellio), 1548
5. Titian (Tiziano Vecellio), 1533
6. Keynes, 1936/2007, p. 156
7. Kondratiev, 1926/1935, p. 35
8. Krugman, 1980, p. 469
9. Hayes, 2019
10. Grossman & Stieglitz, 1980, p. 404

22. In Business like in Warfare

1. Brosnan & De Waal, 2003, pp. 297-299
2. Oswald & Zizzo, 2000, pp. 2,3,9,13
3. Gatti & Henriques, 2009
4. Standard&Poor's, 2021
5. Bernanke, 1995

Acknowledgments

This book owes much to the encouragement and advice given by my parents, Marcel and Marie-Louise Scheidhauer, and by my wife, Karine Cabrol. Major sources of inspiration were exchanges with Prof. Jean Leca, who supervised my doctoral thesis at Sciences-Po, Prof. Elisabeth Dupoirier, Prof. Marc Lazar, Prof. Renaud Dehousse, Dr. Bruno Palier, Prof. Ronald Hatto, Ralf Kissel, Ludovic Grousset, Prof. Sophie Duchesne (Sciences-Po), Prof. Andrée Tabouret-Keller (University of Strasburg), Dr. Thalia Magioglou (EHESS), Prof. John Loughlin (University of Wales), Dr. Christine Hélot, (University of Strasburg), as well as with Prof. Pascal Chaigneau and Jean-Louis Terrier (HEC).

Dr. Christophe Scheidhauer is a researcher. He initially specialized in political psychology, in semiotics and in sociolinguistics. He lectured in international public law and in political economy. He also worked as a financial analyst, and as a public relation officer. He advises entrepreneurs, investment funds and governmental authorities on innovative projects. He settled in Paris.